# Play Ball!

# PLAY BALL!

by
## JAMES C. HEFLEY
Author of *Living Miracles*

ONDERVAN PUBLISHING HOUSE
GRAND RAPIDS, MICHIGAN

PLAY BALL!
Copyright 1964 by
Zondervan Publishing House
Grand Rapids, Michigan

Library of Congress Catalog Card No. 64-22831

First printing ....... October, 1964
Second printing ... November, 1964
Third printing ..... February, 1965
Fourth printing ........ July, 1965

*Printed in the United States of America*

### DEDICATION AND APPRECIATION

*This book is dedicated to the coaches and players who comprise the Fellowship of Christian Athletes, an organization raised up by God to confront modern youth with a witness of the virile and manly Christ.*

    ❀    ❀    ❀    ❀

*Appreciation is expressed to the David C. Cook Publishing Company of Elgin, Illinois, for featuring many of these articles in* Sunday Digest, Christian Living *and* Looking Ahead. *The articles were written while the author was a member of their editorial staff.*

# INTRODUCTION

Almost every man, woman, or child, is a hero worshiper to some degree, and this book is being published to take advantage of this very fact.

The sixteen men you will read about in the following pages are, or were, V.I.P.'s in the athletic world. The one common denominator of them all is the fact that they belong to, and are active in the Fellowship of Christian Athletes. They are not only good Christians, but they are proud to stand up and tell the world of their strong Christian beliefs.

A constant source of irritation to me is the fact that many people today talk a good game of Christianity, but don't practice what they preach. Others "live by the Cross" but are ashamed even to tell their friends they attend church regularly.

This book is aimed at the youth of our nation, but the adults will profit as well if the advice of these men is heeded. Its purpose is simple — to confront the younger generation, and, especially the athletes, with the challenge and adventure of following Christ in the fellowship of the Church.

I deplore this "win at all cost" attitude that dominates the sports scene today. We of the Fellowship of Christian Athletes remember well Grantland Rice's words, "When the Great Scorer comes to write against your name, He cares not whether you won or lost, but how you played the game."

There is only one real answer to the many problems that confront the world today, and that is Christianity.

A Christian is one who plays any game (whether it be athletics or the game of life) according to the rules, to the best of his ability, and to win. A Christian stays physically, mentally and morally clean. A Christian judges his fellowman not upon color of skin, creed, or religion, but on performance alone.

I know most of these men — some very well — and I know they are Christians and great men. They are great men because they are Christians.

These men give their testimony in order that you might know Christ and, knowing Him, thus believe.

OTTO GRAHAM *
Commander, U. S. Coast Guard Academy,
New London, Connecticut
Head Football Coach and Athletic Director

* All-American and all-time great quarterback at Northwestern University, Evanston, Illinois. (1943 — year he was All-American.) In one game against Michigan he completed 20 of 29 passes.

Listed on all-time great team of professional Cleveland Browns. As a pro he never failed to lead either his division or the entire circuit in passing. QB for Browns. While playing professional football he passed for 174 touchdowns in two leagues.

Retired from playing in 1954 but was enticed back to play for the sagging Browns in 1955 when the team ran into trouble. He picked them up and led them to another championship, then *climaxed his career by scoring two touchdowns personally and passing for two more against the Los Angeles Rams in the championship game.*

For a time after his retirement he lived in the Cleveland area but for the past six years (before 1964) he has been both athletic director and football coach of the United States Coast Guard Academy. Each August he steps back into the national limelight by directing the College All-Stars in their annual battle with the defending pro-champions.

Has long been active in the Fellowship of Christian Athletes.

Many sports writers think of him as the "greatest football quarterback" ever to play college and professional football.

# PREFACE

Here are the stories of sixteen star professional athletes. Millions have watched them perform. Some of them are better known to American youth than the President. The crack of a bat, the thud of a caught ball, a touchdown pass, a bone-jarring tackle — and the crowds have roared for these rugged men.

Sports writers have poured millions of words into newspaper hoppers to describe the successes and occasional failures of these top athletes. But the best news of all about these sports champions has — for the most part — gone untold. This is the news that these sixteen — and many other star athletes — are dedicated Christians.

Now that I have met them, prayed with them and written their stories, I shall never be the same again.

Listening to Coach Paul Dietzel lead his Army football team in a before-breakfast prayer — seeing the Bibles in Felipe Alou and Juan Marichal's hotel room — hearing an All-American football player say modestly, "My strength and ability comes from Christ" — these have been experiences that I will never forget — experiences that are presented to you in this book.

As you read you will ask, as I have, "What makes these athletes so dedicated — so different from the average church member? Why do they go 'all-out' for Jesus Christ? Why do they take such a strong stand against the vices in modern living?"

The answer is simply that they are *committed to win*. As professional athletes, they must put out not 90%, but 100% to stay in the game. By discipline, desire and practice they have leaped ahead of thousands of other athletes to become champions. And their desire and discipline has carried over in their Christian living. They understand — and live — the meaning of the word *commitment*.

They are committed to win — on the playing field and in the game of life.

# CONTENTS

Introduction

Preface

# 1

## PAUL DIETZEL

God's Man at West Point

**Head Football Coach: U.S. Military Academy**
*Little All-American center and captain, Miami (Ohio) University, 1946; Coach of the Year, LSU, 1958; Called "the most successful football coach in America."*
*Home: Mansfield, Ohio.*

As THE ARMY TEAM huddled, the cadets in the stands sizzled a long "Sh-h-h-h-h." Then when the huddle broke and the team lined up against the Air Force Academy, the time bomb exploded. "Go, Army, Go!" shouted thousands of voices.

The scene was Soldiers Field in Chicago — November 2, 1963. The two service academies were battling before 72,000 fans and a regional television audience of millions.

Tension mounted as the game moved on. Air Force took the lead in the second quarter with a field goal; then Army stole it back with a touchdown. But the Falcons bounced back in the third quarter to go ahead 10-7.

Now it was the fourth quarter. Army had marched to the Air Force 17-yard stripe. It was fourth down and still two yards to go. The clock showed less than two minutes to play. "Go, Army, go!" the hoarse cadets shouted. On the Army sideline, the slim blond coach with the boyish face peered anxiously across the field as his team lined up. Paul Dietzel knew that *this* was *the play.*

13

Dietzel's quarterback, Rollie Stitchweh, pitched out to Left Halfback Ken Waldrop who was running to his right. The halfback scooped in the ball, slanted off right tackle and seconds later plunged through the Air Force line for the winning score.

After the game, Paul Dietzel — called "the most successful coach" in America — relaxed with a soft drink and talked. "Many more like that and I'll be an old man long before my time," he said flashing his best smile.

No one around believed him. For at 39, Paul Dietzel looked more like 29. But no one suggested that his youthful looks belied his coaching ability. This was the coach who before coming to Army had piloted Louisiana State University's football team to a national championship — the coach known for his tough discipline, but the coach whose team prays before every game, "Lord, protect us and our opponents from injury. Help us play clean, follow the rules and honor You."

Recently Paul Dietzel appeared on the NBC-TV *Today* program and startled millions of viewers with his unashamed Christian testimony. "Life for me has taken on new meaning since I committed my life to Jesus Christ," he said quietly. "Before that I was blinded by materialsm. I had everything I thought worth living for, yet there was still an emptiness. I felt as if I were on a treadmill going nowhere. Then in 1959 I was invited to speak at a Fellowship of Christian Athletes' conference in Estes Park, Colorado. There I realized I had only been living the shell of the Christian life. I felt I must completely give my life to Christ or quit pretending. I did surrender to Christ and now, four years later, I wonder why I waited so long to give up some so called 'modern things' (such as social drinking). What I have given up the Lord has replaced a thousandfold."

Coach Paul Dietzel has surprised and inspired many by his no-holds-barred Christian testimony. But he is quick to admit that before his commitment at Estes Park the Christian life was for him an on-again, off-again experience.

When a child he professed faith in Christ in the Fremont, Ohio, Evangelical and Reformed Church. After his parents were divorced he drifted from church attendance. He earned clothes money setting pins in a bowling alley, then in the ninth grade lied about his age to get a job in a meat market. He spent most of his spare time in a pool room.

But Anne Wilson came along and Paul fell so hard that he changed his hanging-out place to meet her ultimatum: "I won't date you if you hang out in a pool room!"

From then on Paul's Sundays started with church and Sunday school at First English Lutheran Church in Mansfield, Ohio — Anne's church — and continued with dinner at the Wilsons, followed by an afternoon with Anne. "Anne's folks practically raised me," he fondly recalls. "When I needed guidance most, they took me under their wings."

In 1943, Paul enlisted in the Air Force and earned his wings as a bomber pilot. He promptly married Anne, then rushed back to the South Pacific and flew twelve bombing missions over Japan before returning to the United States to attend "lead crew school."

After discharge from the Air Force, Paul enrolled at Miami (Ohio) University where he earned good grades, supported Ann with a butcher's job at the "Veteran's Village Store," captained the football team, and made Little-All-American center in football during his junior year.

Shortly before graduation he applied for entrance into Columbia University's medical school. He was all set to enter but a call from West Point and some advice from his old service chaplain caused him to switch careers at the last moment.

The ex-chaplain was Rev. Pat Murphy, pastor of Walnut Hills-Avondale Methodist Church in Marietta, Ohio. Pat had served Paul Dietzel's bomber squadron during the war and had not been aware that Paul was close by until he read a sports story lauding Paul's football prowess. When Pat called to renew their acquaintance, Paul was eager for some advice.

"Army wants me to be their freshman football coach," Paul told him. "I can't decide whether to accept or to go on to medical school."

"I'd take the coaching job," Pat Murphy advised. "There's

no one in the community who can have more influence than a football coach."

Paul took his old chaplain's advice and joined the West Point Athletic staff in 1948. From here on he moved up and around fast in the coaching world. In 1949 he went to the University of Cincinnati; in 1951 to the University of Kentucky (as Bear Bryant's assistant); back to West Point as an assistant coach in 1953; then to LSU in 1955 where he spent seven years before becoming Army's head football coach.

His LSU team lost the first six games in their 1956 season. Local sports' pages headlined, *If Dietzel loses one more game, he will set a record for LSU*. The poor showing drove Dietzel to his knees. "Lord, pick me up by the scruff of the neck and give me the strength to do my job," he prayed. He started attending services more regularly at the University Methodist Church and took the job of head usher. At the end of the unsuccessful season, an assistant coach told him, "I don't see how you kept your poise with the newspapers and everybody else constantly on your neck." Paul Dietzel replied humbly, "You don't know how weak I was."

At LSU Dietzel acquired the reputation of being a tough coach. He allowed no deviation from training rules. When players let their grades drop, Dietzel put them in a compulsory study hall. But his toughness built a football dynasty at LSU and took the school to the top of national ranks. His LSU teams journeyed to three major bowls in four years while he was in Baton Rouge. In 1958 Dietzel was elected "Coach of the Year." The year before he hadn't received a single mention from 597 coaches in the "Coach of the Year" voting. In 1958 with his "Number One" team he was first, second or third on 475 of 618 ballots.

No one was surprised when Paul Dietzel was invited to become head football coach at West Point. "I did a lot of praying before asking LSU for a release from my contract," he recalls.

The school reluctantly gave Dietzel his release, although some reporters accused Dietzel of betraying LSU. Dietzel in his quiet, unbelligerent manner said simply, "Five years ago

LSU invited me here and asked Army to release me from a line-coach contract. Nobody fussed then. I guess turnabout isn't fair play."

Dietzel is now in his second year as Army's head football coach. Many think he will build a team comparable to some of Army's great teams of the past.

The coach quarters his family (wife Anne, Steve 13 and Kathy Ann 9) in a comfortable home provided by the academy. The Dietzels attend Sunday school and church at the Cadet Chapel. "The cadets teach our kids in Sunday School," he says. "They're wonderful teachers. Ann takes care of the flower arrangements at the altar and arranges the dozens of Chapel weddings that come every June.

"We have a lot of things the world calls success, but our greatest riches are in Christ. We enjoy a wonderful family life. But why shouldn't we? We're Christians.

"I know I'll never regret committing my life to Christ as Lord and Saviour. With His help I'm winning the greatest battle in life — victory over myself.

"When you become a Christian," the coach continues, "God sweeps your house clean, but webs and dirt will keep coming back. I've found that I must constantly battle against temptation to keep myself under control. Some of the 'sidetracks' are very appealing. Before, I used to say to myself, 'I'm having too much fun to give this up,' but I found that a Christian gives up nothing worthwhile and gains everything that counts.

"A coach once told me that every disciplinary problem he has had started from drinking. When I thought about this, I realized this was true in my experience. So I gave up drinking and naturally do not permit my players to indulge. Anyway, what would a boy think if he should see me — a professed Christian and coach of a great team with a drink in my hand? In my book, drinking, smoking and immorality work together to undermine the athlete.

"When I surrendered my life to Christ, I pledged myself to measure my actions and plans by the Life and Person of Christ. But I've found that I can't discipline myself by myself. I only strangle when I start to pull myself up by my own neck. I must have help from Above."

Paul Dietzel voices a strong personal conviction about the manliness of Christ. "Too many people think of Jesus as sweet, tender, meek and mild — an effeminate weakling," he says. "But I don't believe this for a minute. Look at Jesus. As a carpenter He did hard manual labor — without modern power tools. Everywhere He went He walked. Once He fasted for 40 days and nights to prepare Himself for His work. He overthrew the money-changers in the temple. He was tortured by the soldiers and made to carry a heavy cross. He hung for six hours in awful agony without a word of complaint. How weak He makes all of us by comparison.

"Neither do I think of the Christian as a weak person. Meekness does not mean weakness. The Bible teaches that the Christian should live a harnessed, self-disciplined, self-controlled life. I have pledged to submit my body as a living sacrifice to Jesus Christ. As an athlete and leader I try to be what I ask my players to be."

Currently Coach Paul Dietzel is serving as President of the Board of the Fellowship of Christian Athletes. He believes strongly in the organization that brought about a revolution in his own Christian life. "Here in America athletes are treated as heroes," he notes. "They have a tremendous following. Many people turn to the sports page first in their newspaper. An athlete — whether coach or player — is in a tremendous position to witness for Christ.

"A fellow-coach impressed this upon me a few years back when we were talking about a talented football player. 'He's a terrific leader,' I said. 'Yes, but so was Al Capone,' my friend replied. Then I realized that leadership ability is not enough. The life must be channeled.

"And this is what we're seeking to do through the Fellowship of Christian Athletes — channel the leadership abilities of athletes into becoming witnesses for Christ through their individual churches. We challenge them to be top-notch Christians all the way."

Besides coaching and talking about practical Christian

living, Paul Dietzel has another talent that shows up on posters around Army's campus. Before the big Navy game it may be, "Mothball the Fleet," with appropriate art work by the coach. To pep up players he may remind them, "When the going gets tough, the tough get going." To challenge players to do their best, he may suggest, "The only difference between a champ and a chump is 'U.' What do 'U' want to be?"

When speaking in FCA conferences his messages are sprinkled with challenging epigrams. In challenging youth to commit themselves to disciplined Christian living, he may say: "Good fellows are a dime a dozen; the aggressive leader who has the courage to say 'no' is the priceless person," or, "What you give, the world has; but what you keep is lost forever."

But perhaps Paul Dietzel's most striking statement of all is his summation of his own Christian testimony: "The greatest decision I ever made was to surrender my life to Jesus Christ."

# 2

# BOBBY RICHARDSON

The Yankee Glue-man
Who Sticks to His Beliefs

**Second Baseman: New York Yankees**
*Holder of many World Series records;
"Outstanding Player" of 1960 World
Series; Youngest player ever elected
as Yankees' "Player Representative";
Called "The glue that keeps the Yan-
kees together."*
*Home: Sumter, South Carolina*

THE YANKEES AND PIRATES were locked in battle for baseball's world championship. Both had won a game and now in the first inning of the third game, the Yankees had loaded the bases. To the plate came Bobby Richardson, the shortest man on the Yankee squad.

During the regular season in similar situations Casey Stengel had put in a pinch hitter for Richardson. This time Stengel let Bobby stay in, giving him the bunt sign on the second pitch. But Bobby fouled this off and ran the count to three balls and two strikes.

On the next pitch Bobby swung hard.

Fifty million television viewers heard the *whack* and watched the ball soar up and into the stands. The Yanks little man had hit a grand slam home run — only the seventh in World Series history.

But more was yet to come. In that third game, Bobby batted in two more runs, giving him a total of six RBI's, a

Series record that topped Joe Di Maggio, Babe Ruth and Lou Gehrig.

The sports writers called Bobby "the mouse that roared." Altogether in the big Series, Bobby hit a blazing .367, which included two triples, two doubles and the big homer. His superb fielding was highlighted by catching a pop foul while he bounced into the stands.

But in spite of Bobby's incredible performance, the Yankees lost the 1960 World Series in the ninth inning.

Manager Casey Stengel bemoaned the loss but poured out praises upon his star second baseman. *Sport* magazine named Bobby "Outstanding Series Player," and awarded him a new Corvette.

"We can't win 'em all," Bobby said simply. "I just thank God for giving me the ability and opportunity to play."

Bobby was voicing a philosophy he had learned from his father. Eleven years before, at 14, Bobby was playing in the American Legion program. His team was competing against a Legion team from Richmond, Virginia, for a sectional championship. On a key double play the umpire ruled that Bobby had not touched second base. Richmond won the game by one run and the next day the local newspaper cited second baseman Bobby as the "goat" of the game.

Five thousand people, including Bobby's parents and neighbors, had seen the "goat" play. "I'm sick about it," Bobby told his father.

"Son," his father said calmly, "when two teams are playing a game, one has to lose. You can't win them all."

"I brooded a long time over that game," Bobby recalls. "But later I learned that dad's philosophy was the best. No team — not even the Yankees — can win every game. But the game of life is different. Because I'm on the right team, I know I'll always be winning there."

No one doubts that Bobby is winning in the game of life. Ralph Houk, the Yankees new general manager, says, "Bobby plays at the top of his game. He plays as though it never is work."

"I feel the Lord has put me in baseball," Bobby says, "and

it's a joy to me because my purpose in living goes beyond the ball diamond."

Bobby joined the winning team and acquired His purpose in living when he was 12. Here's what he says about it:

"Our family attended Sunday school at Grace Baptist Church in Sumter, South Carolina. One day the minister, Reverend J. B. Simpson, visited our home. He read John 3:16, 'For God so loved the world, that he gave his only begotten Son, that whosoever believeth in him should not perish, but have everlasting life.'

"He talked to me for over an hour about what it meant to believe and become a Christian. Then I knelt in prayer and asked the Lord to forgive my sins and come into my life. A few days later I publicly announced my commitment in church and was baptized.

"From this initial commitment to Christ, I date the beginning of my real purpose in living. My goal is not to win fame in baseball, but to live a life of knowing, loving and walking daily with Christ. This I believe makes me a better player."

Bobby's initiation into baseball came several years before his conversion. His father worked long hours building tombstones, but Bobby remembers that "he was never too tired to play catch with me when he came home from the shop."

Down the street from the Richardson's home lived 19-year-old Harry Stokes. Harry had played some in the minors. He first taught Bobby how to make the "double-play" for which Bobby has since become famous.

A next-door neighbor brought home a Philadelphia Phillies game program to Bobby. "It became my dreambook," Bobby says. "I almost worshiped Phillie stars like Robin Roberts."

When he was only seven, Bobby played catcher in the Sumter "Knee-Pants League." Three years later he joined a Salvation Army team — still a catcher. By the time he reached 14, he was good enough to play on Sumter's American Legion team. During the three years that Bobby played Legion ball, the team won two regional championships.

H. P. Dawson, the business manager for a nearby Yankee

farm club, saw Bobby playing Legion ball and jotted his name down as a likely prospect. When Bobby finished high school, the Yankees were waiting with an invitation for a tryout in New York. Bobby went and the Yankee management agreed that Bobby was a "likely prospect." They immediately signed him as a $3,000 bonus player. Today, Yankee General Manager Ralph Houk declares he wouldn't take less than $3,000,000 for the quartet of Yankee infielders to which Bobby belongs.

But in those days Bobby was a long way from becoming a vital cog in a three-million-dollar infield. He remembers his start in professional baseball as "one of the toughest times in my life."

Bobby's first assignment was with the Yankee farm club at Norfolk, Virginia. He left Sumter by bus and arrived in Norfolk at five A.M. on a cold, cloudy day. Ahead of him was an unknown future.

"I was just a green kid," Bobby says, "lonesome and homesick. I was nervous and scared at playing with experienced older men. A few letters from home cheered me up, but the big boost came from my old high school coach, Conley Alexander. He wrote about how lonely he had been while in service. Then he challenged me to make this verse of Scripture a reality in my life: 'Seek ye first the kingdom of God and his righteousness and all these things shall be added unto you' (Matthew 6:33).

"I re-dedicated my life to the Lord, but my playing continued to be terrible. Then the Yankees re-assigned me to a lower classification club and I began to do better.

"I began three long years of apprenticeship in the minors, playing for clubs in Binghamton, New York; Richmond, Virginia; and Denver, Colorado. At Binghamton, I was challenged once again to honor God in my baseball career.

"Before he ever arrived, I heard some of the guys talking about Johnny Hunton. They said he was a fanatic and a 'holy joe' because he didn't curse, drink or smoke. But when I met Johnny, I liked the way he stood up for what he believed. He didn't let the guff of a few players get him down. By his courage, he challenged me to take a positive stand for Christian living, even if it meant criticism from other players. Now after 11 years in professional ball, I know that athletes respect the guy who is sincere and stands up for what he believes."

Bobby's big break came in 1956 when he was promoted to the Yankee roster. He came into the majors tagged as "the best infield prospect in the minor leagues." But when he wasn't allowed to play regularly, he became discouraged. "I wondered if I should remain in baseball, unless I could play regularly," he recalls. "I became tired of living out of a suitcase and longed to be back home with my wife, Betsy."

Bobby had met Betsy several years earlier in Sumter's Grace Baptist Church. "We sat across the aisle from each other," Bobby says with a gleam in his eyes. "One Sunday after the benediction we got acquainted in the aisle. She looked at me with her big blue eyes and that was *it*.

"While I was considering leaving baseball, I walked the streets trying to decide what was God's will. I prayed constantly for His guidance. I hoped I would get traded to a team on which I could play regularly. But then a Yankee player was injured, opening up a spot for me.

Bobby's first full year with the Yankees was 1957. He batted .256 but played only a few minutes in the World Series against Milwaukee. By 1959, Bobby had raised his batting average to .301, the highest of all Yankees that year. In 1960, he hit his famous grand slam home run in the World Series. In 1961, his .391 World Series average topped all other players in the five games it took the Yankees to beat Cincinnati for the world title.

In 1962, Bobby compiled a .302 batting mark and was the only player in the American League to make over 200 hits. In 1963 his batting average dropped to .265, but he was good enough to earn a third straight slot on the American League All-Star team picked by *The Sporting News.* This was the year in which his ex-manager, Casey Stengel, picked Bobby for his All-Star squad from all the players who had played for the Yankees while Casey was manager.

Baseball enthusiasts say it's hard to tell which Bobby is best at — hitting or fielding. Bobby's roommate, Tony Kubek, says, "Bobby's just about perfect in making the hit and run, and he's an exceptional base stealer, too." Yankee General Manager Ralph Houk calls Bobby "everybody's kind of ball player." Other baseball authorities have called Bobby "a manager's dream player" and "the glue man that holds a team together."

What does Bobby say about himself? "The source of my skill and power is in Jesus Christ. Pleasing Him is more important to me than being a great ball player."

Because of his playing ability and Christian witness, Bobby is in great demand to speak before church and youth groups. He has spoken to 12,000 young people at the Washington, D.C. Capital Teens Youth for Christ Convention and recently to 8,000 more young people at Winona Lake.

Bobby often receives letters from church people asking why he plays on Sunday. "The question of Sunday baseball is something every Christian player has to work out for himself," he says. "I think that if you're in doubt, you shouldn't play. But I'm not in doubt. Through baseball I can serve and witness for Christ. I'm able to go to church before a Sunday game, and incidentally, I've never yet heard of a manager penalizing a player because he came to the park late after attending church.

"I feel that God has put me in professional baseball. I play for His glory and not for the fame that comes from being a stadium hero. The crowds on earth soon forget the heroes of the past. But God never does forget those who believe in His Son. I wouldn't trade my 'name' with Him for every famous name on earth."

# 3

# BILL
# WADE

Signal-Caller for Christ

**Quarterback: Chicago Bears**
*At Vanderbilt University voted South-
eastern Conference's "Most Valuable
Player" by coaches in 1951; Los Angeles Rams, 1954-61; Led NFL passers, 1962; Named "Best Quarterback
in Western Division of NFL" by The
Sporting News, 1962, '63; Quarterbacked Chicago Bears to NFL title in
1963. TV sports personality in Nashville, Tennessee.*
*Home: Nashville, Tennessee*

FORTY-SIX THOUSAND FANS shivered in ten-degree weather and
screamed, "Go, Bears. Go! Go, Bears. Go!" Over fifty million others watched via network television.

This was pro-football's game of the year. At stake was
the 1963 National Football League championship. Contending
were the Chicago Bears (champs of the Western Division
NFL) and the New York Giants (winners of the Eastern Division title).

Now in the third quarter the Bears possessed the ball on
the Giants' 13-yard stripe. But the Giants were ahead 14-10
and it was third down and nine to go. A three-point field goal
wouldn't help the Bears. They had to go for broke.

Bill Wade, the wavy-haired Bear quarterback, took the
brown football and faded back to pass. Bear Mike Ditka

26

charged into the secondary and Wade plunked a "slant-in" pass into Ditka's arms.

Ditka took the pass on the five and ran to the one-yard-line. Two plays later Bill Wade, the quarterback, dove into the Giant line on a quarterback sneak for the score that proved to be the title-winning touchdown.

Not in 17 years had Chicago won a championship. In the dressing room, the awed, thankful team shouted and sang their praises of Coach George Halas. Coach Halas, breaking with emotion, gave credit to his players, including Bill Wade. "Bill played a great game," the wiry old coach said simply. "He led us to the championship."

Bill Wade, in his calm modest manner, talked about the five pass interceptions made by the Bear defense. He praised his teammates on the offensive squad. But everyone knew that Wade, the steady, gallant performer had done his job, too. For him, the dream of ten years in professional football had come true. He had quarterbacked a team to the top.

But what many fans and sports writers did not know was that Bill Wade's greatest victory had come 11 years before — not on a football field, but on a naval vessel anchored in the harbor of Bremerton, Washington. It happened this way . . .

After graduating from Vanderbilt University Bill had been called into the Navy through the Reserve Officers Training Corps. One evening he was in his ship cabin, writing a letter home, when another officer abruptly appeared at the door.

"Pardon me," the stranger said, "I must be in the wrong place. I was looking for Dusty Rhoades who is in the Officers' Christian Union." Then noticing a Bible on Bill's writing desk, he added, "Are you a Christian?"

"Well, I think I am," Bill drawled.

"Would you like to know for sure?" the visiting officer asked, before introducing himself as Jim Wilson.

That started a six-hour conversation about whether or not Bill could know if he was a Christian. The following evening the two ensigns met again for another six-hour Bible study session.

Recalling the conversation that led to his life-changing

decision, Bill says, "Jim went through the whole Bible with me. I told him I believed Christ was the Son of God. But Jim kept emphasizing a personal acceptance of Christ. This was a fresh thought to me. I had been brought up in a fine church and had come from a fine family. Christian doctrines had been taught to me and I had accepted them. I also taught Sunday school back home in Nashville. But through Jim Wilson I realized I needed to personally receive Christ into my life.

"I would ask questions and Jim would flip through his Bible to find the answer. He read to me John 3:16, 'For God so loved the world, that he gave his only begotten Son, that whosoever believeth in him should not perish, but have everlasting life.' Then he asked me if I would accept Christ as my personal Saviour and pray for Him to come into my life. But being a stubborn fellow, I refused.

"Throughout the next week I thought a lot about our talk. I re-read the Bible verses Jim had showed me. But I was hesitant about making a personal commitment. We Wades are known to be the go-slow type who want to make sure of things before we leap. But finally I did ask Christ to come into my life and be my Lord.

"This didn't cause a really great change in my outward life. I had lived a pretty clean life before. But when I accepted Christ, there came an inward peace and thirst for spiritual things. I began to pray and study the Bible more than I ever had. Thankfulness to God for His grace became the motivating force in my Christian service. There has been a steady spiritual growth with me and a real love for truth in all walks of life."

Not long after Bill's personal acceptance of Christ, he was directed to another person who would mean much in his future life.

He was playing on a Navy football team and shortly before a big game was asked to pose for publicity pictures. When Bill met the photographer he found that Sharon Townsend, the beautiful sandy-haired queen of the game, was also to be in the pictures.

Bill was injured later and put in the hospital in San Diego, California. While there, an admiral's son asked him if there was "a particular girl" he'd like to date. Bill remembered the game queen. "Yes. How about Sharon Townsend? Do you know where I could call her?"

Bill called Sharon. That date initiated others, and the following spring, Bill and Sharon signed a contract with each other for life. They now have three children: William III 9, Don 8, and Lisa 4. "We are a happy Christian family," Bill says. "Sharon is a wonderful Christian mother and wife."

Before entering the Navy, Bill had been the first college player picked in the National Football League player draft after the 1951 season. When he finished his Navy time, he reported to the Los Angeles Rams.

While at Vanderbilt Bill had earned many athletic honors. His junior year, he had ranked fourth among all major college passers in the nation. His senior year, he had captained the Vanderbilt team, led the Southeastern Conference in total offense, was voted the Conference's "Most Valuable Player" by a poll of coaches. He was also selected "All-American" by the *Chicago Tribune* and picked as a second team All-American choice by the Associated Press.

Bill's first years in pro-football were frustrating for him. In college he had been accustomed to playing regularly, but for four years he sat on the sidelines, going in only as an occasional substitute for the regular quarterback, Norm Van Brocklin. Then in 1958 Van Brocklin was traded to the Philadelphia Eagles, and Bill was given the starting quarterback slot. That year, Bill set Ram records for pass attempts (341), passes completed (181) and yards gained in passing (2,875). His yards gained were only 63 yards short of Sammy Baugh's National Football League record.

Yet despite Bill's stellar performance, the Rams alternated him as quarterback with Frank Ryan during the next two seasons. In 1961 Bill was traded to the Chicago Bears, but here again he found another quarterback ahead of him.

Not until 1962 did Bill become the regular quarterback of the Bears. That year he led all National Football League

teams in pass completions (225). He was chosen "best quar-
terback in the Western Division of the NFL by *The Sporting
News,* an honor repeated in 1963 when the Bears won the
NFL championship.

During the frustrating years when Bill played second-
fiddle to other quarterbacks, he continued to be a faithful
Christian. Once Bill was criticized by a sports writer for
talking softly in a Los Angeles game. The scribe thought
Bill could be more effective if he used profanity. A California
fan read the criticism in the papers and wrote her sympathy.
Bill wrote back his appreciation. Her future letters revealed
her spiritual need. Several letters later Bill helped her to
trust in Christ.

Another sports writer reported that Bill had cursed after
a game. A young boy read the story and wrote Bill, asking
if it were true. Bill gave the boy a firm denial, then called
and reminded the writer of his responsibilities and asked for
a retraction. The writer admitted his error, printed a retraction and is now a friend of Bill's.

Because he has been misquoted and misrepresented several times, Bill dislikes publicity. He believes that some sports
writers belittle him because they do not understand the life
he lives. But he respects the power of the press. "The press
has tremendous power," he says, "and all journalists — especially Christians — should be careful to print the truth. Quotes
should be quotes, not figments of imagination."

Bill prefers individual contacts in Christian witnessing
to speaking before large audiences. "One good personal contact for Christ is better for me than speaking to fifty million
people," he says, although he speaks frequently to church
groups and others interested in athletics. He answers fan
letters personally, except those requesting pictures. To many
he sends his photo with John 3:16 inscribed across the base.

He serves on the Board of Directors of the Fellowship
of Christian Athletes and helps direct FCA activities in his
home town of Nashville. Here, during the off-season, he has
been featured on *Bill Wade Sports,* a weekly, 25-minute tele-
cast over WLAC-TV. When Yankee second baseman, Bobby

Richardson, came to Nashville for the kick-off dinner of the Fellowship of Christian Athletes, Bill interviewed Bobby on his TV program. They talked about baseball and the reason for Bobby's visit to Nashville, which gave Bobby an opportunity to declare his faith in Christ.

Easter week-end, 1963, found Bill with several other Christian athletes in Daytona Beach, Florida, for the annual influx of partying college students. They did not come to participate in the spree, but to confront the students with a face-to-face Christian witness. "It was the greatest experience of my Christian life," Bill says. "It was so exciting that I hardly had time to eat or sleep. All week it seemed miracles happened as God used me to remind students of their spiritual lives."

Bill has accepted invitations to speak to Knights of Columbus clubs in the Chicago area. What does he, a Presbyterian, say to Roman Catholic men? "I talk about my Christian faith the way I would at any religious meeting," Bill answers.

In Chicago and across the country, Bill's name has become a household word among pro-football fans. Boys are frequently asking him, "What does it take to become a great football player?" To which Bill, when speaking to youth groups, sometimes answers with this acrostic:

"C — *Confidence*. You, your coach and your teammates must have confidence in your ability. If you're a Christian you can have confidence in God: '. . . If God be for us, who can be against us' (Romans 8:31).

"H — *Humility*. There's never been a team that won every game. In athletics you must learn to lose. Neither do you always win in life, but God will teach you through setbacks to depend upon Him. Learn to benefit from your losses and then forget them. Don't spend 50 years of your life pouting over a failure. There's always another game.

"R — *Respect*. Respect a fellow for what he is. In pro-football we don't care what race a player is who makes a touchdown. Personally, I think pro sports clubs have been among the first groups to make concrete progress toward racial equality. As Christians we *must* respect others regardless of their race or background. The Bible says plainly that 'God is no respecter of persons' (Acts 10:34).

"*I — Intelligence.* It takes a vast amount of work and study to keep up with football. I study more now than when I was in college. The mental preparation is much harder than the physical. A Christian should study and be intelligent if he is to be useful in service for Christ. We are to be 'wise as serpents' and 'harmless as doves.'

"*S — Sincerity.* I must be sincere if my coach is to believe in me. As a Christian, I must be sincere if people are to believe what I say about Christ.

"*T —.Truth.* In football, films tell the tale. Often someone will ask me after a game, 'What happened on that play?' I will reply, 'I can't say for sure until I've seen the films.' God has a film of your life and you are responsible to Him for everything you have done, even your innermost thoughts. A Christian can face the truth. So to God and to all you meet, be true."

Bill's acrostic, of course, spells out Christ. And He best explains the consistent life and witness of Bill Wade, quarterback of the Chicago Bears, champions of the National Football League for 1963.

# 4

## FRANCIS TARKENTON

"P.K." in a Tough Slot

**Quarterback: Minnesota Vikings**
*All-American Academic Team, University of Georgia, 1960; Led Southeast Conference in passing and total offense, 1960; Sensational rookie quarterback for Vikings.*
*Home: Athens, Georgia*

THE YOUNG SOUTHERNER with the innocent brown eyes and boyish wave in front looked about as harmless as a ministerial student duded out to preach his first sermon. When he arrived in Minneapolis, some thought he looked "too nice" for the rough and tumble game of professional football.

But Coach Norm Van Brocklin of the Minnesota Vikings had selected Francis Tarkenton after studying movies of 25 college quarterbacks in action. Soon after Fran arrived, the Dutchman coach sent him in to quarterback an exhibition game against the Dallas Cowboys. The 21-year-old "Cracker," as the coach called him, pulled his helmet over the wavy lock, huddled with his team to explain the play, then took the snapped ball and bounced back behind his line seven yards. From a protective pocket formed by Viking linemen, he peered through the wave of charging Cowboys, spotted his receiver and zipped the ball through for the touchdown.

A few weeks later "Fancy Fran," as he was then being called by sports scribes, quarterbacked his first league game

33

against the Chicago Bears in the Vikings home stadium. Time and again Fran was hit hard by Bear linemen who got through the protective pocket. But he bounced back to pour enough short passes over Bear heads to lead the Vikings in winning 37-13. Altogether, Fran threw four touchdown passes and scored one TD himself by rushing. When he came off the field, Coach Van Brocklin greeted him with tears of joy.

Fran Tarkenton at 23 is easily the most sensational young quarterback in the National Football League. At the end of the 1961 season he was runnerup to Mike Ditka of the Bears as National League "rookie of the year." During the 1962 season Fran threw 22 touchdown passes — the Vikings scored only seven more by rushing — and ranked fifth in the National Football League in passing yardage with 163 completions for 2,595 yards. One of his pass completions was for 89 yards against the Bears — the longest pass completion of the NFL season in 1962.

But above and beyond all his success on the gridiron, Fran Tarkenton is a "P.K." — a preacher's kid — who is proud of it, and who has not deserted his father's faith.

When Fran came to the Vikings in 1961, two months after graduating with honors from the University of Georgia, word got around quickly about his ancestry. Mayor Petersen of Minneapolis introduced Fran at a Viking Club banquet as the "new P.K. on our squad." For his teammates, coaches and fans, Fran Tarkenton has been "P.K." ever since.

"I've had to live up to those initials all my life," Fran says. "The name is an honor. I've always been very proud of my father. Sure, some people think a preacher's son is a pushover — especially in sports. But dad always wanted me to build a strong body — said my body was the temple of the Holy Spirit. Like most preachers, dad never made a big salary. He couldn't buy me expensive sports equipment. But he encouraged me to be active in sports at the "Y." My desire to excell in sports was kindled and nurtured in the "Y" Junior Leagues."

Fran's athletic ability blossomed rapidly after he entered high school in Athens, Georgia. Here he was all-state in basketball, baseball and football, and in his junior year he led the Athens football team to a state championship.

A flock of colleges dangled scholarship bait before him, but the methodical Fran coolly compiled information on each college, then ranked them first, second or third, according to what they seemed to offer. Then his dad came in to ask, "Have you prayed about which college to attend?"

Fran hadn't, so he went to his room and knelt to ask God's guidance. Fran remembers the experience as a clear answer to prayer. "When I got up off my knees, I knew God wanted me to go to the University of Georgia, even though this school had been third on my list of preferences. Later I understood why, for there I met my wife and also led in organizing a chapter of the Fellowship of Christian Athletes."

At Georgia, Fran quarterbacked the freshman team to an undefeated season. But his best call during his freshman year came when he asked a blue-eyed, 5′ 3″ majorette for a date. Fran and Elaine Merrell — also a freshman had their first date at the First Baptist Church of Decatur, Georgia, and they've been going to church together ever since.

Fran played on the varsity squad during his sophomore year, then in his junior year he quarterbacked the squad to the Southeastern Conference title and they were ranked number five in the 1959 Associated Press College Football Poll. That year he set an accuracy record in the Southeastern Conference by connecting on 60.8% of his passes. The team also went to the Orange Bowl where Fran led Georgia in defeating Nebraska 14-0 with 29 and 33-yard touchdown passes.

Georgia's P.K. quarterback continued his stellar performance during his senior year. He led the Southeastern Conference in passing and total offense and ranked fifth in the nation among collegiate passers. He was named to the Associated Press' second All-American team and was also picked on the All-American Academic team because of his high grades. At the end of his college career, his record showed he had completed 186 of 317 passes for 2,100 yards and 18 touchdowns, plus gaining 229 yards on the ground and scoring 10 more touchdowns.

Thus when he finished college Fran was expected to become a star on the pro-circuit. Some also expected that in pro-football Fran would drift from the moorings of his faith.

When he joined the Vikings, a player commented caustically, "We've seen others like you, kid. They come into pro-ball good little Christian boys. The first year they start smoking, the second drinking and the third chasing women."

Fran merely smiled and shook his head. His three years are up now and he still holds the line on his convictions. "A Christian shouldn't let people drag him down," he says. "Some guys like to see you down in the gutter with them because it helps them feel better about their own sins."

Since coming to the Vikings, Fran's boyish face has appeared on the covers of two national magazines — *Life* and *Sports Illustrated.* But the publicity hasn't turned his face away from his main goal in life — living and witnessing for Jesus Christ. Fran and Elaine are active members of the Hennephin Methodist Church in Minneapolis. (Fran's father is a Methodist minister.) Both serve on the youth board and specialize in youth commitment and dedication.

Fran often speaks three or four times a week to church and athletic groups. "Sometimes I shock a church group," he says. "They expect me to tell a lot of football yarns. But I use football only to open my message about complete dedication of life to Jesus Christ."

Fran admits that his life hasn't always been fully dedicated to Christ. "I was converted when I was nine," he recalls. "I went forward to an altar and asked the Lord to forgive my sins and come into my heart. It was a real experience. But going into my teens, I began thinking and reasoning more for myself. I respected my folks, but I couldn't be satisfied with believing something just because dad and mother did. Looking back now I can see periods of stagnation, readjustment and growth in my Christian life.

"The great turning point for me came at the Fellowship of Christian Athletes Conference in Estes Park, Colorado, back in 1958. There I heard some of my boyhood heroes speak unashamedly about their Christian faith. Men like Otto Graham and Don Moomaw really impressed me. I knew they had come long distances just to attend the Conference and share their faith in Christ.

"At Estes Park I became aware of my weak and ineffectual Christian witness. I realized that I hadn't surrendered all phases of my life to God's will. I told God that I would give Him my life completely — with no reservations attached. I would go anywhere, do anything as He gave me strength and guidance.

"I came back to the University of Georgia with renewed determination to make my life count for Christ. I began praying more — reading my Bible more — witnessing more. Fellows began coming to my room, asking my motivations in life. About 20 started going to church with me. Then we started a campus chapter of the Fellowship of Christian Athletes.

"Christ's power soon became real to me on the football field. A few months after the 1958 FCA Conference at Estes Park, we were playing in the last seconds of a game against Auburn that would decide the Southeastern Conference championship. Auburn was ahead 13-7. We had moved to their 13-yard line. As the quarterback I had to call a play — but what play? I asked for time out during which I bowed my head and prayed. A play came into my mind that we had never tried before. I explained it as best I could in the huddle. Then we lined up and I shot a pass into the end zone for a touchdown. We kicked the extra point and won the game 14-13.

"I've found great comfort in prayer in pro-football. Last season I was really down after losing three straight games. Many of my passes weren't hitting the target. I just wasn't playing as well as I thought I could. I began praying more every night and morning, asking God to lift the mental pressure. He lifted the burden and gave me renewed strength and presence of mind.

"But I never pray to win a game. As a quarterback, I pray for strength to lead my team well . . . to do my best . . . to enjoy presence of mind. Prayer isn't a 'rabbit's foot.' A Christian isn't necessarily 'lucky' just because he prays. I don't bargain with God and say I'll go to church and give my time and money if He will help me win football games. I believe in going to church, but for me, Christianity is an all-week-long affair.

"Jesus never promised victory or success as the world views success. But He did promise strength for living and victory over death at the end of this life. When I'm playing a game, I know that all my strength and wisdom comes from Him. God gave me the talent to play and I want to use it to bring more people to Christ. Some say that a Christian in professional athletics is only 'making a name for himself.' But my purpose goes beyond self-glory. People listen to me when I talk about Christ because of my 'name.'

"I enjoy the challenge that football offers," Fran says enthusiastically. "You're always pressing toward a goal, striving to win over opposition. When I fade back to throw a pass I have to watch the running pattern of my receiver. I can't worry about the opposing linemen that are trying to muscle past my blockers and pull me down. Likewise, I've found that in the Christian life I have to keep my eyes on the goal — witnessing for Christ. A Christian can get so pre-occupied with watching out for the tacklers of evil that he takes his eyes off life's main purpose. I think Paul had something like this in mind when he said, 'I press toward the mark for the prize of the high calling of God in Christ Jesus' (Philippians 3:14).

"Football has also taught me that I can't go it alone. When I take the snap from center and fall back to pass, my blockers try to keep the opposing linemen from getting to me while I'm trying to get the pass away. Without these protectors I would be a sitting duck to be smeared for a big loss.

"Along this line I think a Christian should take all the outside help he can get. My primary strength comes from Christ as I yield myself to Him and let His purposes be lived out in me. But I also receive strength from worship and fellowship with other Christians at church."

Fran is quick to add that he is "no isolationist." "I believe in mixing with all people — Christians or not," he says frankly. "Didn't Jesus spend more time with sinners than He did with religious people. In pro-football I'm not playing with a bunch of choir singers. A lot of the guys drink and do other things I don't believe in. But we travel together on road trips and when some of the guys have alcoholic drinks, I take a coke and sit beside them. I want to show them that a Christian can enjoy life — without liquor. I want them to see the love of Christ in me. After all, that's why I'm in pro-football — to be a witness for Christ. And that's what really counts."

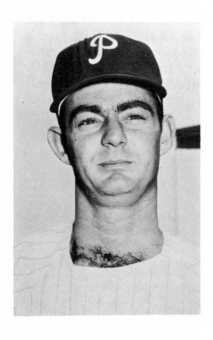

# 5

## DON DEMETER

Versatile Big Leaguer
on the Victory Side

**Outfielder: Detroit Tigers**
*Formerly star second baseman, Philadelphia Phillies. Led Phillies in batting with .307 and 29 home runs in 1962; Top defensive player of the National League in 1963, playing 119 games without committing an error; Played for World Champion Dodgers in 1959 World Series.*
*Home: Oklahoma City, Oklahoma*

THE NATTILY DRESSED big leaguer spoke intensely as we sat in the plush lobby of Chicago's Edgewater Beach Hotel. "I've had some great thrills in my career," he said, "like hitting three home runs in two different games, batting .307 in 1962 with 29 homers and 107 RBI's. But the greatest was the World Series in 1959. We—I was playing for the Los Angeles Dodgers, then — beat the White Sox. The thrill of winning was pure ecstasy. It was a baseball player's dream come true."

Then he paused and said huskily, "But for me, winning the Series does not compare with the thrill of being a witness for Christ."

This was Don Demeter talking. He's a rangy six-feet-four Oklahoman with 195 pounds of rippling muscle and solid physique. He stands tall in the saddle on horseback, tall at the plate in a big league ball game, and is a big leaguer who can handle five positions with ease — first and third base and the three outfield posts.

A few hours before I had seen him perform against the Chicago Cubs. In the third inning a Cub batter slammed a burning line drive toward left field. Demeter, playing third base, leaped like a mountain lion to snare the ball and spoil a hit.

It was the top of the fourth and Demeter was up to bat for his Phillies team. He ambled loosely around the plate, taking a few practice swings. The pitcher threw hard. Whack! It was a line drive to left field, a base hit.

Then it was the fifth and the Phillies were at bat again. Two men were out and the bags were jammed with Phillies when Demeter came up, swinging his bat and looking relaxed. The Cub crowd began chanting to their pitcher, "We want an out! We want an out!" Sportscaster Jack Brickhouse called the rangy Oklahoman "a dangerous man." And so he proved to be.

He swung at a fast ball — strike one. The pitcher threw again. Pow! — another sharp liner to left and two Phillies raced across the plate. The season was a month from being over and Don had put in the record his 68th and 69th RBI for the year.

Came the seventh inning, and the Cubs loaded the bases. Cub batter Lou Brock hit a long floating fly ball to center field. Demeter was there — he had been moved from third base to center field. He reached up and pulled it down.

Unfortunately for the Phillies the Cubs took the game seven to six — but through no fault of Don Demeter who had turned in another stellar performance.

Now at the hotel Don told about his "greatest win of all." He was only twelve and living with foster parents. His foster father, George Stevens, was and still is Sunday School Superintendent at the Exchange Avenue Baptist Church in Oklahoma City. Don was impressed and inspired by the Christian testimony of the Stevens' family. "I watched the way they lived both at church and at home, during good times and hard times," he said. "Through them I could see that the Christian life was truly worthwhile. On Easter Sunday, 1947,

I walked forward at the close of the church service to sign a lifetime contract with Jesus Christ my Lord and Savior. Today, 16 years later, I've forgotten the preacher's sermon, but I've never forgotten the Christian example the Stevens' family lived before me."

Two years before, Don had started his baseball career in the Oklahoma City YMCA Junior League. In high school his team won the State title in 1953. Every player on the squad, except Don, was named to the All Oklahoma City High School Baseball Team.

But a Dodger Scout pegged lanky Don Demeter as big league timber and signed him for the 1953 season to play with the Dodgers' Class D farm club in Shawnee, Oklahoma. Don's salary that first season was $150 a month.

Don played center field and hit only .223 his first year in the minors. Still he was sent up to Bakersfield, California, a Class C club.

That year he heard about Alvin Dark, tithing his World Series earnings to his home church in Lake Charles, Louisiana. "I knew that if Al Dark could tithe his Series money," Don said, "then I could tithe my $150 a month. Later in 1959 I had an opportunity to tithe my own share in the Series."

At Bakersfield Don's batting average zipped up to .270 and he swatted 28 home runs. His Dodger owners moved him on up to Fort Worth.

One memorable summer week-end the Fort Worth club came to Oklahoma City to play Don's home town club. On Sunday morning Don went to his church at Exchange Avenue Baptist. He sat down in the pew beside his foster-brother, Bill Stevens, and looked toward the minister and choir. "Who's that cute blonde?" he asked Bill.

"Don't you remember? You went to high school with her."

"Not little Betty Madole?"

Bill Stevens nodded.

"Get me a date with her for the game tomorrow night," Don requested eagerly.

Bill arranged a double-date. Don went on ahead to the

ball park to suit up. Bill Stevens and the two girls were scheduled to attend the game and meet Don afterward.

Throughout the first four innings Don watched for his friends to come in the stands. Don saw them come in just before going to bat in the fifth inning. He slammed a hard double off the left field wall. His next time up he connected with a home run. The stands rocked with cheers. Don swelled at the thought of how impressed his date would be.

With the game over, Don swaggered toward the spot where his date was sitting. He was anticipating a "you-were-really-super-tonight" greeting. But as he climbed the stands the girl seemed not to notice him.

Don felt perplexed. Then the truth leaked out when Bill Stevens said, "Betty, this is Don Demeter, your date for to-night."

"Oh, hello Don," the blonde said casually. "I had forgotten what you looked like. Been so long since we were in high school together."

But during the months ahead Don impressed Betty Madole enough to persuade her to say yes when he proposed. Today Don and Betty have two future ball players of their own; five-year-old Russ and two-year-old Todd. When they're home Betty sings in the choir at Exchange Avenue and both teach Sunday school.

In 1956 Don was called up to the Dodgers as a pinch hitter. His first year in the majors he only batted three times. The first time he struck out against Vinegar Ben Mizell of the St. Louis Cardinals; the second time he hit a homer off Vinegar Ben. Today Don counts Vinegar Ben as one of his dearest Christian friends.

The next season Don was sent back to the minors to play for St. Paul, Minnesota. The following year he came back to the Dodgers. During the 1959 season he helped the Dodgers win the National League pennant and the World Series against the Chicago White Sox. This was the year he had the privilege of tithing his World Series earnings.

In 1961 he was traded to the Philadelphia Phillies, the club for which he played through 1963. His best year in

Philadelphia came in 1962 when he led the team with a .307 batting average, 29 home runs and 107 runs batted in. At the end of the season he received 12 votes for the Most Valuable Player Award in the National League.

During the 1963 season Don hit .258 with 22 homers and 83 runs batted in. Several of Don's homers came at crucial times. On June 25, Don hit his 15th homer off Harvey Haddix, famed Pittsburgh pitcher. The home run broke up a tie game in the tenth inning and gave the win to the Phillies. Playing defense, Don topped all other National League outfielders in 1963. He played 119 games without committing a single error.

Don Demeter is respected among major leaguers, not only as a ball player, but also as a Christian with strong personal convictions. He does not drink, curse or smoke. "I know that some Christians smoke," he says, "but I agree with my friend, Vinegar Ben Mizell. Ben says, 'Smoking may not send a fellow to hell, but it makes him smell like he's been there.'"

Don also turns down the easy money offered to athletes for endorsing brands of beer and cigarettes. "I teach a class of 15-year-old boys back home," Don says resolutely, "and if they saw my name under a cigarette or beer ad, all my teaching influence would go out the window. Besides I would be lying to endorse something I neither use nor believe in."

When asked if he found it difficult to turn down a cocktail or bottle of beer, Don replied grinning, "Not really. For me there's no decision to make in refusing a drink of alcohol. I made that decision when I dedicated my life to Christ."

Don admits that he was only a "nominal Christian" until he realized how much his influence could count for Christ. Speaking invitations from men and boys' church groups have poured in. He has received dozens of letters from admiring youth and grateful parents who express their "appreciation for the Christian stand you take."

Even during the regular season Don attends church whenever possible. One Sunday he may go to church in Chicago; another Sunday in New York, wherever the team happens to be playing. And during his free months they are at home in

Oklahoma City where Don teaches his boys' Sunday school class.

Don confesses that he has his ups and downs. "The Christian life is a lot like baseball," he says. "Our team will hit a winning streak, then our fortunes will change and we'll start losing. But when I'm down in the Christian life I've learned to pull on the latch strings of heaven.

"Living in the limelight makes a Christian ballplayer easy prey to pride," he adds. "But a guy will learn a lesson in humility.

"I think of the time I was playing for the Dodgers against Milwaukee. We were leading the Braves by one game in the National League pennant race with a week to go in the season. In the bottom of the ninth we were ahead by a run. Don Drysdale was pitching for us. The Braves had a man on second with two outs. The batter hit a fly ball to me in center field. I called for it, ran under and reached up. The ball bounced off my glove and by the time I had picked it up the runner had scored. That tied the game. We finally won in fifteen innings, but no thanks to me. On the way to the hotel I shook every Dodger's hand on the bus, expressing my appreciation of 'the team's win.'

"At the end of the season we tied with Milwaukee for the pennant, but won out in a playoff. I felt mighty thankful and grateful to play in the World Series that year. My error could have lost us the World Championship."

Don has had his share of minor injuries in playing ball. "An athlete must learn to live with them," he says. In 1960 Don broke his wrist in a game against Pittsburgh and was out for half of the season. "But this was good for me," he says. "When I got home my church was having a summer revival. The revival gave me a spiritual lift. That summer's rest built me up spiritually and made me stronger for the next year's play."

In talking to church groups Don uses illustrations from athletics. "As a professional athlete I must live a disciplined life," he says. "This means regular hours of sleep and proper food. I can't eat just anything. If I break my physical discipline my ball playing shows it. It's the same with my spiritual life. I must feed it and grow in grace through Bible study, prayer and witnessing.

"Learning to play five positions on the baseball diamond, has taken long hours of practice. I've had to follow the rules and listen to my coaches. The Christian life is like that. One must keep doing the spiritual disciplines over and over and listen to the 'Master Coach' if he is to be a top-notch Christian.

"A Christian," Don continues, "can be likened to a ball lying on the center of a ruler. If the ruler is tilted up the ball naturally rolls down by force of gravity. To roll up, the ball must have someone pushing it. I've found that I need the Lord's strength behind me if I'm to keep going up in the Christian life."

Don Demeter is still going up in baseball circles. But he's also advancing in the Christian life. Perhaps one big reason is as Don says, "Baseball isn't my first love. It's only my occupation. My first love is Christ. My greatest desire is to be an effective witness for Christ. If I should be taken out of baseball tomorrow through injury or otherwise, my life wouldn't end. I know that God would have something else for me to do for His glory.

"But this doesn't mean that I don't play to win every game. We Christian athletes have the greatest desire to play because we play for the glory of God. I play just as hard against a Christian friend who happens to be on the opposing team as against anyone else. Take Bobby Richardson of the Yankees. If Bobby was on second base and I was a base runner sliding in, Bobby would expect me to come in hard, and I would. But I wouldn't spike him. There's a way to hit a baseman hard with your legs or knees and make him lose control of the ball — without spiking him."

In February, 1963, Don and Bobby teamed up to witness for Christ. They went to Japan under the sponsorship of the Texas Baptist Convention to participate in the "New Life Campaign." Don recalls this as one of the great spiritual experiences of his life. "The Lord's hand was on me," he says fervently. "Three days before time to leave I wasn't sure I could go. My passport hadn't been cleared and I hadn't signed my player's contract for the next year. I called the missionary who was directing the campaign and told him I couldn't go. Then a call from Tokyo said my passport was okay. And my general manager, John Quinn, called a few minutes later and we made a contract agreement over the telephone."

In Japan Bobby and Don gave their Christian testimony to crowds of curious young people. They spoke to Japanese baseball players in two major leagues. Just before leaving they held a news conference during which they re-emphasized their purpose in coming to Japan. "We are two Christians from the United States," they said. "We are here to present our witness for Christ."

And that pretty well sums up Don Demeter's purpose in life. Not just to play baseball, but to witness for Christ.

(After this article was finished, Don Demeter went to the Detroit Tigers in a trading swap. During the 1964 season, Don is expected to play a key role in bolstering Detroit's pennant hopes.)

# 6

# RAYMOND BERRY

The Man of a Million Moves

**Offensive End: Baltimore Colts**
*Starred in NFL Championship Play-off between New York Giants and Colts in 1958; All-Pro End 1958, '59, '60; Played in Pro Bowl 1958, '59, '61, '63; Third ranking pass receiver in NFL with a career total of 6,217 yards.*
*Home: Paris, Texas*

THE COMMISSIONER of the National Football League called it "the super-colossal game of them all."

The place: Yankee Stadium in New York. The time: December 28, 1958. The teams: The New York Giants, champs of the Eastern Division, NFL vs. the Baltimore Colts, champs of the Western Division, NFL. At stake: The championship of the National Football League.

During the first half, Johnny Unitas, quarterback of the Colts, mixed running and passing to direct the Colts to a 14-3 lead. But the Giants came roaring back in the second half to wipe out the Colt lead and go ahead 17-14.

With less than two minutes to play, the Colts lined up on their own 15 for a last-ditch try. They had 85 long yards to go for the winning score. Johnny Unitas tried two quick passes, but both fell incomplete. Then on third and ten he hit Lenny Moore for 11 yards and a first down. The precious seconds were ticking away and there was still 74 long yards to go.

Back came Unitas to throw a short pass downfield. Raymond Berry, No. 82, took the ball about six yards deep and ran for 25 more. The clock ticked on. In rapid succession, Unitas threw two more passes downfield to Berry, who had finished the regular season tied for first place in pass receiving. "Mr. Gluefingers" scooped in the ball both times. Now the Colts were on the Giants 13 with seven seconds left in the game. But this was enough for Steve Myrha of the Colts to kick a field goal, tying the score at 17-17, and sending the game into the first "sudden death" overtime in pro-football history.

In the overtime period Unitas, Berry, Moore, and company used four completed passes and strong running gains to carry the Colts to the Giants one-yard stripe. Colt fullback Alan Ameche surged over for the score and the championship belonged to the Colts from Baltimore.

After the game someone was talking to Giant owner Jack Mara about Raymond Berry's amazing catches. "Berry can hardly see," the man marveled. "He has to wear powerful contact lenses. How could he catch so many passes?"

"Uh-huh," grunted the Giant owner. "That Berry can't see anything but footballs."

Now five years later, Raymond Berry, who can't even see the big E on the eye chart, is still seeing footballs extremely well. Mr. Gluefingers holds almost every pass receiving record for the Colts. In eight years he has scooped in enough balls to make 6,217 yards — enough to give him third ranking in the NFL — only Billy Howton and Don Hutson are ahead. In the NFL he is one of only 13 receivers to ever exceed 1,000 yards in a single season.

Tom Brookshier, former star with the Philadelphia Eagles, recalls a game in which Berry caught 10 balls. "Berry is almost impossible," Brookshier says. "He has every fake there is."

Sports writers galore have lauded Berry's sticky fingers. *Life* magazine featured a two-page spread (December 7, 1959) on "the surest hands in pro-football." One *Life* picture graphically showed only the hands of Berry as they were spread wide to receive a pass. *Life* pointed out that one Berry finger has been dislocated five times.

Raymond, who looks and acts like a mild-mannered assistant college professor, credits his pass-catching ability to "the ability and the opportunity to work, practice and play given me by God."

Those who know Raymond hold only respect for his willingness to work hard. He weighed only 150 pounds when he finished high school in Paris, Texas, where his dad was football coach. So he enrolled in Schreiner Institute for a year of junior college football. That year he caught 32 passes for eight touchdowns — enough to catch the eye of Southern Methodist University. At SMU, Raymond played very little until his senior year when he excelled in defense and was co-captain of the Mustangs.

The Baltimore Colts drafted Raymond for a pass-receiving slot. "They were building a team from the ground up and couldn't be too choosy," Raymond says modestly. "When I returned for my second year of pro-ball, I felt my chances of staying on the team were very poor. The Colts were looking for another end to replace me. The pressure on me not to flub up during a game became almost unbearable.

"For the first time in my life, I lost confidence in my ability to catch a football. It was a new experience for me for I had always had confidence in my hands and catching ability. The mental tension was terrible. Playing football had become my whole life. To fail to make the team seemed to me then to be the end.

"I remember one terrible experience vividly. During a game, I broke wide open for a deep pass down the middle. I was so afraid I would miss it that my concentration was ruined, and I did miss it. I felt my world ending and visualized being cut from the team at the end of the game. I experienced the feeling that I knew drove some people to suicide."

The record books show that Raymond Berry's pigskin career did not end in 1956. That was the year Johnny Unitas and Lenny Moore came to the Colts — "the two greatest athletes I have ever known," according to Raymond. Raymond, himself, worked hard, running pass patterns with Unitas, practicing running with the ball, squeezing a ball of putty regularly to build strength into his hands and studying game films constantly.

Then with Raymond Berry at left end, Lenny Moore at right flanker, Jim Mutscheller at tight end, and Quarterback Unitas throwing the passes, Baltimore won the NFL championship in 1958 and 1959. For three successive years — 1958, '59, '60 — Raymond was chosen All-Pro end. Raymond, in his typical modesty, gives credit to his teammates who provided "marvelous pass protection, strong running by Alan Ameche and L. G. Dupre, and the best defense in the NFL."

Something else happened to Raymond Berry during this time when he was becoming the most widely acclaimed pass receiver in professional football. Raymond tells about it in his testimony, written especially for this story.

"During the period '57-'60, though I was not greatly aware of it at the time, a change was taking place in my life. I began to consider the many, many blessings in my life. I felt a need to pray and say 'thanks.' I also felt a compulsion to read the Bible and find out what was in it.

"Reading that a good wife is a 'gift from the Lord,' I began asking God to select my wife. That prayer was answered in the spring of 1960 when God brought my wife-to-be, Sally Crook, and me together. We met at Baylor University while I was coaching there and she was a senior student.

"I also felt that I should contribute to the needs of missionaries as I remembered a verse from childhood, 'Go ye into all the world and preach the gospel.' I began asking God to help me do my part in that. I didn't know then that I needed a missionary myself, or that Don Shinnick, my teammate on the Colts, was the missionary God would send to me.

"You see, I had been brought up attending church and Sunday school. At some point in my childhood I came to believe that Jesus was the Son of God. When I was about 10 years old I was baptized. And my attendance at worship services had always been regular. I believe this is partly the reason why I didn't understand what Don was talking about when he first began to speak to me about Jesus Christ.

"Don and I had been good friends since he came to the Colts in 1957. But he never said much to me about 'religion' until the summer of 1960. Sally and I were engaged at the time. Don and I were at Fort Meade, Maryland, on a two-week summer camp with the National Guard. One evening we were talking about Christ and Don said, 'Raymond, I don't believe you have ever accepted Christ as your Saviour.' He wasn't telling me what he knew for sure, but just what he thought. I didn't understand what he meant by 'accept.' I just assumed that believing Jesus was God's Son made me a Christian.

"About a week later we talked about Christ again. I'm still not sure just why I prayed as I did that night. Somehow I just felt that this was what God wanted me to do and at that stage in my life I wanted to do what He wanted. I asked Don to help me pray, then I told God I wanted to put my complete faith and trust in His Son as my Savior. I asked Him to forgive my sins and to help me understand what I was doing. Don had assured me that if I trusted Jesus the Holy Spirit would then live in me, help me understand the Word of God and give me strength to live for and glorify Christ. Not having heard this before, I didn't understand it, but then I didn't doubt it, either. Don read to me I John 1:9, the scripture that tells Christians what to do about daily sins. He encouraged me to confess these whenever and wherever I was aware of them.

"The changes that took place after that were gradual, day by day, a little at a time. For the first time I began to realize what a sinner I was. Prayer became an everyday experience. Studying the Word of God became a real joy, and verses that before had no meaning suddenly did have meaning. As I looked back to where I stood in the sight of God before that July night when I prayed, there gradually came the awareness that *I had been a lost soul.* Before then Christ had not meant any more to me than any other person in history. There had been no connection in my mind between Jesus Christ and salvation or even what salvation meant. And I don't ever remember wondering just *why* Christ came into

the world, and *what* is the significance of His life, death and
resurrection. I can only say now that I am *so* thankful to Him
for saving my soul from the eternal fire and letting me know
that He loves me."

Raymond has given his Christian testimony many times
since he accepted Christ in 1960. But he will always remember the first opportunity.

The squad was flying home after a game. A sports writer
traveling with the squad was interviewing Raymond for a
feature story. The opportunity came for Raymond to tell about
the most important thing in his life, when the writer asked
for a written statement of Raymond's faith. "I was just a
new Christian and was still trying to understand myself what
was the significance of trusting Christ, so I went to Don
Shinnick to get some help," Raymond recalls. "Don suggested
that I simply tell what had happened to me spiritually. So
as best I could and with some help I wrote out a statement."

After the season Raymond was invited to speak at a church
brotherhood banquet. A husky telephone linesman eagerly
grabbed his hand. "You helped a friend of mine become a
Christian."

"How?" Raymond asked.

"He has always been a real Colt fan. I have been en-
couraging him to put his trust in Christ. Reading what you
had to say in the newspaper article really impressed him and
gave me another opportunity to talk to him. Not too long
ago he decided to trust Jesus as his Savior."

"My life hasn't always been smooth since that July night
in 1960," Raymond admits. "The daily struggle with diso-
bedience, lack of trust, self and sin never lets up. It seems that
failure is constant, but thanks be to God for the cleansing blood
of His Son and for being able to take everything to Him in
prayer. To know that the Holy Spirit lives within and will
handle things when left in charge is such a great assurance.
Yielding and trusting and obeying is my problem. I just ask
God for grace to do these things.

"Back in '62 I was benched for about half the season.
Logic told me that the coach had nothing personal in mind

but was just trying to help the team get rolling. But logic didn't keep the thoughts of hate and resentment from my heart. I would ask the Lord to forgive me but two seconds later the thought was back. This seemed to go on for weeks, but gradually things changed for the better. It was an experience that brought to me new understanding of Romans 7:14-25.

"In the second game of last season my shoulder was dislocated. At first it appeared I might be sidelined for the entire season. I thought that perhaps I was being disciplined for something. But very quickly God gave me peace about it and I felt no worry at all. The shoulder healed very quickly and I was able to return to the lineup for the last seven games of the '63 season."

Injuries or not, sports experts expect Raymond Berry to be around the pro circuits for a long time, scooping in passes, then running, jumping, shifting and faking his way for long gains. Indeed, Mr. Gluefingers may very well set an all-time pass receiving record before taking to the showers for the last time.

Called "the man of a million moves" and "the greatest faker in football," Raymond pulls no fake when he says, "The greatest 'move' in my life happened when, by God's grace, I put my complete trust in Jesus Christ as my Savior and Lord. I used to think life was exciting as a pro-football player, but living day by day with the Lord and knowing He will help me in everything is wonderful. Most people are 'hep' on happiness, but there is only one source of happiness and that is Christ. There is only one source of peace and that is in Him. The Lord will change you if you'll let Him. He is the answer, the *complete* answer to every problem on earth."

# 7

## FELIPE ALOU

A Bat—a Bible—and a Brave

**Outfielder: Milwaukee Braves**
*In 1962, led pennant-winning San Francisco Giants in batting with a .316 average and 25 home runs. Home: Santo Domingo, Dominican Republic*

SMILING, DARK-SKINNED Felipe Alou met me at the door of his hotel room. "Come in," he said softly. "Sit down and we will talk."

Felipe sat down easily on his bed. He wore tan trousers, sharply creased, and a light tan polo shirt that accented his brown eyes. His arms looked smooth-muscled and strong. They had batted .316 and led the San Francisco Giants in hitting during 1962. They had made the hit that became the winning run in the Giants-Dodgers pennant playoff of '62.

I glanced at the table beside Felipe's bed. The usual ash tray filled with cigarette butts was missing. In its place was a Bible. On the table beside the other bed was a second Bible.

"My roommate, Juan Marichal's," Felipe said softly. "We both read the best Book in the league."

A moment later Juan Marichal, the 25-game winning pitcher for the Giants, came in. I stood up to shake hands. Behind Juan trailed Orlando Cepeda, Jose Pagan and Felipe's younger brothers, Matty and Jesus (pronounced Yesu). All were Giants and Latins. For a moment I felt like a foreigner in the American city of Milwaukee where the Giants were playing that night. I would have felt like a missionary, except I knew my host was an effective missionary himself. After his teammates left, Felipe mentioned modestly that one Latin teammate had already trusted Christ.

How had Felipe, an obscure boy from the Dominican Republic, reached the major leagues? More important, how had he become a missionary with a ball and bat?

In excellent English, edged in a Latin accent, Felipe told me how his dreams had come true.

Felipe was born and raised in Santo Domingo, the capital of the Dominican Republic. His family was poor but devout Roman Catholics with high moral standards. They lived in a small wooden house to which Felipe and his brothers carried water from more than a mile away.

During one school vacation Felipe had worked on his uncle's farm, rising at midnight to begin an 18-hour work day. Another summer he worked in a concrete plant for $14 a week. Even spearfishing — one of his favorite sports — was used to earn extra income. Felipe and his brothers speared and wrestled sharks, then sold the oil from the sharks' livers.

Felipe was a model boy. Relatives and neighbors predicted he would become a priest or a great doctor. He went to confession and communion regularly. He was an honor student and a star baseball player at Santo Domingo High School.

After high school graduation Felipe enrolled in the premed course at the University of Domingo. At the university Felipe played baseball and also went out for track and field. He went to the Pan American games in Mexico where he threw the javelin and ran in the 100 meter race.

When Felipe returned home from Mexico, an invitation to sign a contract with the San Francisco Giants was waiting. Since his family needed money, Felipe took the advice of the university athletic director, Horacio Martinez, and signed.

The Giants sent Felipe to their farm club in Coca Coca, Florida. His first year, Felipe led the Florida State League with a .380 batting average. At the end of the season he returned home a hero.

A crowd met him at the airport, bringing expensive gifts and shouting their admiration. Later, when the crowd had left, a boyhood friend came to see him. Rocque Martinez and Felipe had been schoolmates and had worked together one summer.

"Well, Felipe, I do not have the money to buy an expensive present," Rocque said. "But I would like to give you this Book. It tells about One who waits to be your best Friend." Then Rocque told how he had become an "evangelical" while Felipe was away playing baseball.

Felipe thanked his old friend and put the Bible in a suitcase where it stayed for five months. Why did Felipe wait so long? "I feared my family's disapproval," Felipe says, "but one night in a motel in Springfield, Massachusetts, I began reading. I started in Genesis and by the time I had reached Matthew, I realized that Jesus Christ had died for the world—even for my sins. But I hesitated to accept Christ as my Savior. I was afraid this might hurt my future in baseball."

When Felipe returned to Santo Domingo at the close of the 1957 season, Rocque was eagerly waiting. "Are you reading the Bible?" he asked Felipe. "Have you become a believer?" Felipe answered evasively and during his remaining time at home he sought to avoid seeing Rocque.

But when Felipe returned for the '58 season he carried Rocque's Spanish Bible with him. He played a six weeks season for Phoenix, then was moved up to Seattle's Triple-A club. Finally in early June his big break came. He was called to San Francisco to play big league ball for the Giants.

June 8 was the day Felipe was scheduled to play his first big league game. But the game was rained out. And Felipe stayed in his hotel room reading telegrams and receiving phone calls of congratulations from his fans in the Dominican Republic.

His eyes grew misty when he looked at a long telegram from his old friend, Rocque Martinez:

"Congratulations, old friend.  Happy for you.  One
of my prayers has been answered.  I'm still praying that you'll believe. Remember, even a big league
ball player needs Christ.  You'll find that baseball
is not everything.  'Be not wise in thine own eyes:
fear the Lord, and depart from evil' (Proverbs
3:7)."

Felipe knew it must have cost his poor friend a half week's
wages to send the long telegram from Santo Domingo to San
Francisco.  He dropped to his knees, asking God to show him
how to become a Christian.

The next day the Giants played and Felipe got a hit his
first time at bat.  Then the team took to the road.  "I met the
big names of baseball," Felipe says, "but I soon discovered
that they had troubles like everyone else.  I knew that Rocque
was right — that baseball wasn't everything."

Now Felipe was reading his Spanish Bible at every opportunity.  Al Worthington, a Giant pitcher, noticed Felipe
pouring over his Bible in a hotel lobby.  "That's a good Book
—the best," Al told Felipe, as he sat down beside him.  Then
he asked Felipe, "Are you a Christian?"

Felipe shook his head.  "No, but I'm going to be one, when
I understand how."

After that Al and Felipe studied the Bible together often.
Felipe said that he believed, but could not feel that Christ had
accepted him.

The team came back to San Francisco for a string of home
games.  In his room at the Whitcomb Hotel, Felipe meditated
upon Romans 10:13—"For whosoever shall call upon the name
of the Lord shall be saved."  "I have called upon Christ," he
told himself.  "He has promised to accept me."  Suddenly the
light dawned.  "I am a Christian!  I belong to Christ!"

Recalling his moment of assurance, Felipe says, "I felt
happier than on the day when I played my first-league game.
Immediately I wrote a letter to Rocque to tell him his prayers
had been answered.  Then I hurried out to the playing field
to tell Al Worthington."

"I was warming up," Al recalled later, "when I saw Felipe running across the field. The glow on his face told me what had happened. I clasped him around the shoulders. 'You know it now, don't you, Felipe?' Felipe nodded. 'Yes, thank you, I know.'"

The white pitcher from Birmingham and the dark-skinned outfielder from the Dominican Republic stood together arm-in-arm — brothers in Christ.

After the '58 season closed, and Felipe was solidly slotted in the majors, he returned to Santo Domingo. His parents and many of his friends had already heard from Rocque Martinez that Felipe had become an "evangelical." Felipe's mother expressed her disapproval, but then when she saw the new joy in his life, she began telling others, "I'm proud of Felipe. He's a great boy. God is talking to him."

Felipe appeared on a television sports program in Santo Domingo and told about his new faith. Afterward many believers in the Dominican Republic wrote to say how happy they were that the country's baseball hero had become an "evangelical."

Rocque Martinez took Felipe to the Biblical Temple in Santo Domingo — a Plymouth Brethren church — where Felipe was received into membership. Felipe's membership is now in the Biblical Temple, although he usually attends Baptist churches in the States during the baseball season.

Felipe's conversion has not hindered his big league career. He has steadily risen to become one of the leading hitters and outfielders in the National League. During 1962 Felipe not only led the pennant-winning Giants in batting (.316), but smashed 25 home runs. Felipe played almost every game during the season. His manager, Alvin Dark, declared, "I can't afford to let him rest." Perhaps Dark was thinking of the time Felipe was injured and the Giants lost seven of the nine games they played without him.

National League managers rate Felipe highly as a runner, fielder and batter. One manager says, "Felipe has the best rightfielding arm in the league." Another notes that Felipe "gets a great jump on the ball."

Felipe feels that with Christ he has a "great jump" on life. "I wish everyone could have the joy that comes through knowing Jesus Christ as Savior and Friend," he says.

The handsome young outfielder from Santo Domingo is doing his part to see that everyone knows. He has led his wife, Maria, to Christ. When he is home they have family altar with their three children: Felipe Jr. 4, Maria 3, and Jose Israel 1.

Between the '62 and '63 seasons, Felipe switched leagues for a few days and went to Venezuela as a lay missionary under the auspices of the Pocket Testament League. He calls this, "the greatest week of my life."

Felipe started the week in the capital city of Caracas where he spoke in the Central Baptist Church. A Caracas newspaper welcomed him with the headline: FELIPE ALOU IN SOUTH AMERICA. Later in the week he spoke in the cities of Porta La Cruz, Cuona, Valencia and Naracay. In Valencia, an industrial center, Felipe threw out the first ball and spoke at a baseball game attended by 9,000.

Reporters crowded about him wherever he went. "Why have you come with a Bible instead of a bat and glove?" they asked. "This Book has the answers to the problems of life," he would reply. Then he would add, "I've had many wonderful thrills in my life, but the greatest came in San Francisco when I trusted Christ as my Savior."

When the whirlwind week was over, missionaries counted converts by the score. As Felipe was preparing to leave, a native Venezuelan said gratefully, "We pray, if God wills, that you will have a great batting average with the Giants. We know that you will have an even greater batting average in heaven."

Recently, a National League manager predicted Felipe will be a .300-plus hitter for several more years. Felipe says, "I'll stay in baseball as long as the Lord wants me there. Through baseball I have an opportunity to win people to Christ.

"Americans for the most part have been wonderful to me. When I played in the minor leagues in Louisiana and Florida,

I felt the sting of discrimination because of the color of my skin. But even in my country things are not perfect. Some have asked me why I do not become an American citizen. I have thought about it. But I love my country, and when I am through with baseball I want to retire there and be a witness for Christ.

"There is a great opportunity for Christians in Latin America now. The countries are going through a social revolution. Communism is gaining in some places, but the real answer is Christ. He is the only One who can stop Communism."

(Felipe Alou went to the Milwaukee Braves in a player swap shortly before this book went to press.)

# 8

# BUDDY DIAL

The Singing Pass Receiver

**Offensive End: Dallas Cowboys**
*All-American, Rice University, 1958;
Set pass catching record at Rice and
also for Pittsburgh Steelers. TV sports-
caster and sacred recording artist.
Home: Magnolia, Texas*

THE PITTSBURGH STEELERS and the Cleveland Browns were playing before 83,000 cheering football fans. The Browns were ahead 7-6 when the Steelers took charge of the ball.

The play was called and Steeler Buddy Dial streaked around the side of the Cleveland line, twisted his lithe body to avoid charging tacklers. Quarterback Ed Brown stepped back and threw a long pass upfield. Dial was there — leaping high into the air to grab the ball for a Steeler first down on the Browns' 43-yard stripe.

A moment later, Ed Brown threw another pass over a wall of rushing Browns. Again, Buddy Dial was there to haul it down — this time on the Browns' 15-yard line.

Another pass to Dial dropped over his head, incomplete. Then the quarterback was smeared for an 8-yard loss by "red-dogging" Brown linesmen. This brought the count to third down and 18 yards to go for the first down. Five yards beyond that point was paydirt for the Steelers — if they could conquer one of the toughest defenses in the league.

The play was barked and Buddy Dial raced to the left sidelines. The QB bounced back for the payoff pass. He threw and the Steelers' star receiver was there waiting. Dial caught the ball in his fingertips behind the goal line and the Steelers went ahead 12-7.

And so it went through most of the 1963 National Football League season during which the Steelers defied the "experts" by landing in the playoff for the Eastern division NFL title. Buddy Dial, who caught 60 passes for 1295 yards and 9 touchdowns, contributed a large portion to his team's efforts to win the title.

Dial doesn't ascribe his pass catching success to mere luck or even to his own ability. He says, "God helped me catch those passes. Before every game I went on the field confident that He would give me strength and guidance."

From a frame house in the river bottom woods near Magnolia, Texas, to All-American and professional football stardom — Buddy has come a long way in his 25 years. For his success he credits his mother whom he says is "the most fabulous Christian I've ever known. She took care of the poor, taught Sunday school and has brought dozens of rural people to Christ. She taught me by example to desire the right things and to pray in faith for them."

After Buddy's older sister was born, the doctors told his mother that she could never have another child. But Mrs. Lee Dial prayed, "Lord, if You'll give me a son, I will dedicate him to You."

What seemed impossible, happened. Five years after this prayer, Mrs. Dial gave birth to a healthy baby boy. When the Dials took Buddy home from the hospital, neither dreamed that he would one day play football in the big city before millions of television fans.

As Buddy grew up, his mother took him and his older sister to the Assembly of God church in Tombull, Texas. Here he committed his life to Christ when he was 12.

"Church activities were all we had to do back there in the woods," Buddy recalls. "We went three or four times a week and it seems we were always having a revival. Sometimes we wouldn't start home until midnight."

The church people predicted a great future for Buddy —

but in Gospel music, not football. Buddy played the guitar well — his dad had taught him — and sang in a clear tenor voice that brought frequent shouts of "Hallelujah," and "Praise the Lord." One of Buddy's most requested songs was, "Life's Railroad to Heaven." As the youthful voice rang out, "Keep your hands upon the throttle and your eyes upon the rail," no one in the church thought that one day Buddy's eye would be upon a football sailing toward him while millions looked on.

But what many football fans do not know today is that Buddy *has* become a recording star. His best-selling religious album, "Buddy Dial Sings," contains many of the old favorites he used to sing in his boyhood church.

As a boy, Buddy was often seen trudging through the woods with guitar under one arm and football under the other. He was constantly asking other boys to play catch with him. At night in his room he would lie on his bed and throw the football in the air for hours at a time. He was developing "eyes" on the tips of his fingers that would later see and grab "impossible" catches.

Buddy's spiritual life developed alongside his football talents. When he was 13 his father worked the graveyard shift at a nearby oil refinery. One night his mother became gravely ill. She stopped breathing. Buddy knelt and cried to God for his mother's healing. As he prayed a voice seemed to whisper, "Give me your life and I will heal her." For a long desperate moment Buddy weighed his purposes in living. He wanted to love and serve Christ, but he also wanted to become a football star. Finally he whispered, "Lord, I give You my life."

Buddy has never forgotten that dramatic moment. "My mother was healed," he says. "She started breathing normally and the very next day was back on her feet."

The test of Buddy's dedication soon came. The football games at his high school were played on Friday night, a church night for Buddy. He had been an outstanding player on the junior high squad and the coach wanted him on the varsity team. "You can go to church on Sunday," he assured Buddy.

But Buddy refused. "I would love to play," he said, "but

my church comes first. I guess you'll just have to do without me."

Buddy remembers that year as one of the toughest in his teen life. "The church people praised me," he says, "but many of the kids at school condemned me. Today as I look back, I believe the Lord was testing my dedication. It wasn't that playing football on Friday night was wrong, but was I willing to put the Lord before football?"

The problem was solved the next year when Buddy's church changed the service time to Saturday night. Buddy played during his last three years of high school and was a standout performer on the gridiron.

During his senior year he began scouting for a football scholarship. His high school was small — only about 100 students — so the chances were slim that a college coach would seek him out. Besides Buddy weighed only 160 pounds. His folks could not afford to send him to college and an athletic scholarship was his only hope of going.

Baylor University was not far from the river bottom where Buddy lived. It was a church school and Buddy felt inclined toward the ministry, so he went scholarship hunting there.

"Too small," the athletic department told him. "We've got only one scholarship left and we're saving it for a bigger man." Buddy then tried for a music scholarship at Baylor, but again to no avail.

But Coach Jess Neely from Rice University heard about Buddy's talents at the tiny Magnolia, Texas, High School. He was willing to take a chance and offered Buddy a scholarship to which Buddy gave verbal acceptance.

A few weeks later Buddy was invited to play in the Texas High School All-Star game. He was the star of the game, making two touchdowns and collecting six passes for 121 yards — a record for the annual All-Star game. The Baylor scouts took note and when Buddy returned home one was waiting. "All you've got to do is sign," the scout told Buddy.

Buddy shook his blond head. "I haven't signed yet, but I gave my promise to Coach Neely *before* the All-Star game. I believe I should keep my promise."

Coach Jess Neely gleefully put Buddy in as a starter for Rice. But in the first quarter of his first college game against Southern Methodist, Buddy injured his knee. A doctor gloomily forecast that he would never play again on the knee. But Buddy's home church prayed for him and the following season he was back practicing with the squad.

Buddy rewarded Jess Neely's confidence by giving a champion performance for Rice. As a sophomore he led the Rice team in scoring and was named the Southwest Conference's best sophomore lineman of 1956. The next year Rice captured the Southwest title, with Buddy making 21 catches for 508 yards to lead the Conference in pass receiving. In the Cotton Bowl on January 1, 1958, Buddy led all the pass receivers with seven passes for 80 yards, even though Navy defeated Rice.

Buddy finished his career at Rice in 1958 with a school record of 68 pass receptions and 13 touchdowns during his three-year career. He was a first team All-America pick by the United Press, Associated Press and the Football Writers' Association.

The New York Giants made him their number two draft choice, but Buddy was dogged by injuries and did not get into a Giant uniform until five weeks after the start of training camp. Even then a Giant coach thought he was "too small," and suggested he "go back to Texas and find a coaching job."

Buddy did not want to give up pro-football, so the Giants put him on the market. Bobby Layne, then the quarterback for the Pittsburgh Steelers, had seen Buddy play in the Southwest Conference. "Grab him quick," he advised the Steeler coaches. They did and for many years the Giants have had reason to regret their mistake.

Playing for the Steelers from 1959 to 1963, Buddy has set the following team records:

— Most yards gained pass receiving, season—1295 (1963).
— Most touchdown passes caught, season — 12 (1961).
— Most yards gained pass receiving, game—235 vs. Cleveland (1961).
— Longest pass reception—88 yards vs. Cleveland (1961).

Also, while playing for the Steelers Buddy became a well-known television personality in Pittsburgh. During the 1962 and 1963 seasons he turned sports announcer before each televised game for a 15-minute "football warmup."

At the close of the 1963 season Buddy became part of a newsmaking trade between the Steelers and the Dallas Cowboys. He is now expected to become one of the top pass receivers for Dallas. How does he view the trade? "Trades are part of a pro-football player's life. I feel the Lord has led me back to Texas to play before the home folks I love."

Smiling, joking Buddy Dial expects to play a good many more years in pro-football. He intends to remain active in Christian work, singing Gospel hymns and speaking to youth groups about his faith in Christ.

He admits that a few of his old neighbors back home still think pro-football is worldly. "What is worldliness?" Buddy asks, then answers his own question. "It is whatever interferes with one's Christian witness. Once I thought I wanted to be a minister, and in a sense that desire has been fulfilled. As a Christian football player I am invited to speak to groups that would not ask a minister. I can — and do — give my Christian testimony to them. Each week during the season I can play before thousands of people who never enter a church, but who come to know what I believe and stand for. Football does *not* interfere with my Christian witness; to the contrary, it broadens my testimony for Christ.

"Now I don't smoke, curse or drink," Buddy adds. "But that isn't the sum total of my Christian witness. I try to live and play so that people will say: 'Here's a Christian who truly enjoys life and plays for a higher purpose than winning a football game.'"

Of course, Buddy's 'higher purpose' is witnessing and living for Jesus Christ. "I am faithful to Christ because I love Him," Buddy says reverently. "Just as I am faithful to my wife, Janice, because I love her."

Buddy and Janice met while he was playing football at Rice. Janice came to the ball game with another boy and through binoculars saw Buddy playing. "I'd like to meet that blond boy who squints his eyes when he's looking to catch the football," she said jokingly. Later she did meet Buddy and from that moment the two became inseparables. Today Buddy and Janice have two sons, three-year-old Darren and one-year-old Kevin.

"Just think," Buddy says with a sly grin, "if I hadn't dedicated my life to the Lord when mother was ill, I might not have kept my promise to Coach Neely. And if I hadn't kept my promise to play for Rice, I might not have met Janice. This is all proof to me that God is working out His purpose in my life."

# 9

## AL
## WORTHINGTON
The Fireman With Faith

**Relief Pitcher: Minnesota Twins**
*Pitched shutouts in first two major
league games; has pitched for San
Francisco Giants, Boston Red Sox,
Chicago White Sox, and Cincinnati
Reds.*
*Home: Birmingham, Alabama*

HE'S A FIREMAN in major league baseball, but he puts out
batters instead of fires. Al Worthington is a relief pitcher,
the man a manager sends in during the late innings to put out
the fire which another pitcher has allowed to spread.

Take last season in Cincinnati when the Reds were playing a home game against the Chicago Cubs. It was the bottom
of the ninth, the Reds were ahead by a single run and two
Cubs were out. Then two Cubs got on base. Ron Santo came
to bat for the Cubs and hit a high hopper toward third base.
The throw was too late. Santo joined his fellow Cubs and the
bases were loaded. Ernie Banks was up next, a Cub not given
to light taps with the bat.

Forthwith marched Manager Fred Hutchinson to the
pitcher's mound. Taking the ball from the tired pitcher,
"Hutch" waved toward his bullpen for Fireman Al Worthington.

Al, a husky six-foot-two, 208 pounder, took his warmup
throws, then settled back to face the Cubs' home run hitter.

He threw three straight balls to Ernie and then a strike. Then with the next pitch, Al put out the fire as Ernie popped up to the Red catcher. Another "save" went into the record books for the veteran relief hurler.

But they aren't all "saves," as Al Worthington and other relief hurlers will tell you. Sometimes the relief pitcher can't keep the fire from getting out of control and the game is lost. About the only thing certain is that a fireman comes to the mound when the tension is running highest.

How does a "fireman" feel coming into the late innings when the score may be tied and the opposing team may have the bases loaded? "I used to feel plenty nervous," the big right-hander from Birmingham says. "With the tension so thick you could slice it, the butterflies would dance in my stomach as I walked to the mound. Knowing that I'm the guy the team is depending on to put out the fire really puts the pressure on me. But the pressure's been off since 1958. Now I walk to the mound feeling calm. The old tight, jittery feeling I used to have is gone. As I walk, I'm praying, 'Lord, help me do my best. Help me keep calm.' I throw the ball knowing my pitching is in the hands of God. I don't make a 'save' every game I pitch relief, but I do walk off the field with peace in my heart."

Al regrets that he waited so long to experience the "big save" in his own life even though he had been a church member since 13. He refers to the day in 1958 when he was on a flying "road trip" from San Francisco to Pittsburgh. "I was reading my Bible," Al recalls, "and came to the verse in John 9:39 where Jesus said, 'I am come into this world, that they which see not might see; and that they which see might be made blind.' Suddenly my eyes were opened. I saw that Christ was my Savior, that He had forgiven all my sin, that in Him I possessed a brand new life. From that moment the Bible became a beautiful Book to me. Christ became a living Presence. The next time I walked to the mound to pitch relief the butterflies were gone from my stomach. Today, I wonder why it took so long for me to realize that Christianity begins with the new birth — not church membership."

Al says that he joined a church on Easter Sunday, 1942. "I was 13," he recalls. "All the other kids joined about that age. I was expected to do the same. But not until 16 years later did I learn that church membership was not enough."

His baseball career began about the same time he joined the church. He pitched four years for the Phillips High School team in Birmingham, then moved on to the University of Alabama for another four years of pitching experience. In 1951 he signed with the Nashville Vols — a minor league team in the now defunct Southern Association. After two seasons, the Giants — owners of the Nashville club — sent him to Minneapolis where he compiled 9 wins and 5 losses. During the last half of the 1953 season he was put on the major league roster as a Giants' pitcher. He amazed the baseball world by pitching shutouts in his first two major league games. In his first start he blanked the Phillies 6-0, allowing only two hits. Five days later he beat the Dodgers by the same score, allowing only four hits.

Al went back to Minneapolis in 1954, still a minor league club, before returning to the Giants in 1956. He pitched four successive years for the Giants — his best year coming in 1958 when he won 11 games and lost only 7. In 1960 he was caught in a trading whirl and was owned by the Boston Red Sox, the Chicago White Sox and two minor league clubs before joining the Cincinnati Reds in early 1963 and becoming the Reds' leading reliefer for the '63 season.

In 1957, early in his professional career, Al began teaching a boys' Sunday school class in Birmingham during the off-season. "I thought I was a pretty good fellow, back then," Al says. "I would talk to the boys about living a good life, then go sit in my pew — third row from the front — drop a big check into the offering plate and relax during the sermon.

"Teaching Sunday school didn't keep me from drinking, although I kept trying to convince myself that I was on the right track with God. But inside I felt a deep, gnawing uncertainty. Billy Graham came to New York — the home of the Giants at that time — but I didn't go. I thought the purpose of the meetings was to reform thieves and drunkards. Both Shirley — my wife — and I felt we were respectable church members, and wasn't that enough?"

In 1958 the Giants moved to San Francisco, and to Al Worthington it seemed that Billy Graham came with them. He and his family had hardly unpacked when they heard about the Graham crusade opening in the Cow Palace.

Al and Shirley decided to go. "But I wasn't particularly impressed by Billy's sermon," Al says. "I just didn't think it was for me."

On their way out of the Cow Palace, Al and Shirley met Bob Speak, a fellow player on the Giants' squad. Bob introduced the Worthingtons to his minister, Rev. Marshall De-Vaughn.

"Hey, you're from the south, aren't you?" Al asked when he heard the minister's drawl.

"From Georgia," the minister replied.

"What are you doing out here?" Al asked.

"I'm recruiting for Christ," the minister answered with a twinkle in his eye. "I'm pastor of a new Baptist church."

"Let's go over to my house and have coffee," Bob Speak suggested. The rest agreed and a few minutes later, the "recruiter" was trying to "sign up" his fellow Southerner.

"But I'm already a Christian!" Al protested. "I belong to a church in Birmingham. I teach Sunday school when I'm home. I hear the preacher every Sunday — sit three rows from the front, and I give as much as anybody else to the church."

The minister-recruiter was not impressed. "What you need, fellow," he told Al, "is to see how bad you really are. Tonight when you pray, ask God to show you the true condition of your heart."

Two days later the Georgia minister came to visit at the Worthington home. Again, Al reminded him of his good deeds and wanted to hear the preacher say he was good enough to go to heaven. Instead, he continued to talk about Christ.

The minister calmly handed his open Bible to Al. "Read right there — verses eight and nine," he suggested.

So Al read, while his wife, Shirley, looked on, "For by grace are ye saved through faith; and that not of yourselves: it is the gift of God: Not of works, lest any man should boast" (Ephesians 2:8, 9).

"See, salvation is God's gift to you," the minister pointed out.

Both Al and Shirley nodded their heads in agreement. "I've been wrong," Al admitted. "But it isn't all clear to me yet. I want to be sure."

"You can be sure," the minister said. "God promises in Romans 10:13, 'Whosoever shall call upon the name of the Lord shall be saved.'"

Al hedged about becoming a Christian that night. But he did promise to hear Billy Graham again at the Cow Palace. This time Al went forward. A counselor talked to him and Al prayed, "Lord, help me understand." But he went away still not sure that he was a Christian. It was on the plane, flying to Pittsburgh for a game with the Pirates, that the light finally broke through. Today Al says, "After I received Christ it seemed so wonderful and so simple that I marvel why it took me so long."

When Al returned from the road trip, Shirley met him at the door with some good news. "The minister and his wife came to see me while you were gone," she said. "I've accepted Christ and I'm so happy."

Right away Al set out to explain to other team members what had happened to him. "One of the fellows thought I had gone off my rocker," he said. "A few listened politely, but I could tell they weren't interested."

But Al soon discovered that at least one teammate was concerned about his spiritual condition. One day Al noticed dark-skinned Felipe Alou, a new player from the Dominican Republic, sitting in a hotel lobby and reading a Bible.

"That's a good Book — the best," he told Felipe.

The big Dominican outfielder looked up anxiously. "A friend back home gave it to me," he said.

"Are you a Christian?" Al asked.

"No, but I'm going to be one, when I understand how."

"Let me help you understand," Al said eagerly.

That marked the beginning of a long friendship between the two teammates.

"Felipe wanted to understand so badly," Al says. "One day I was warming up before a game, when I saw Felipe come running from under the stands. The glow on his face told me what had happened. I clasped him around the shoulders. 'You know it now, don't you, Felipe?' I said. Felipe's smiling brown face bobbed up and down. 'Yes, I know.'

"Felipe had a friend in the Dominican Republic who was praying for him. He had been wanting to become a Christian for a long time. But most professional athletes are not as concerned about their spiritual need.

"An athlete has the tendency to look on the Lord as a crutch," Al believes. "Take a guy who comes into the major leagues as a poor boy and unknown outside of his own community. Suddenly he has money and sees his name in the sports headlines of big city newspapers. He feels self-sufficient, thinks he's a great guy and sees no reason to grab a religious crutch. Year after year his goal is to have a big year and to make more money. Then one day he's injured or becomes too old for baseball. His money and fans are gone. He's left with nothing but old memories.

"My goal as a Christian athlete is to go and do what the Lord tells me to do. He gives me strength from day to day."

What are Al's plans when his time is up in the big leagues?

"Our old world is in pretty bad shape," he says. "It's a lot like a baseball game going into the ninth inning with the evil team threatening to win. Some of the veteran players are getting weary out on the field. They need some relief players. I'd like to go in full time if my Coach should call me. But if my Coach — the Lord — doesn't call me to preach, I'll look for a coaching and teaching position in high school.

"We need to reach the kids while they're young. That's the best way I know to have more Christian athletes — win them while they're young.

"Shirley and I are trying to do that with our children. We've got three, Linda 12, Allen Jr. 9 and Michelle 6. Linda accepted the Lord one night after I read to her Romans 10: 9, 13. Allen Jr. trusted Christ a few months later. We're proud of our kids and want to give them a Christian home.

"I train to keep my pitching arm in trim. As a reliefer, I'm always expecting to be sent into a tight game. That's the way it is with the Christian way of life. Whether I'm at home with Shirley and the kids or away on a road trip, I try to be in top spiritual condition to witness for Christ. A guy never knows when an opportunity to 'pitch' for Christ will open up."

(During the 1964 season, Al Worthington was purchased by the Minnesota Twins to bolster their bullpen staff.)

# 10

# BILL GLASS

The Preacher Who Throws His Weight Around

**Defensive End: Cleveland Browns**
*All-American, Baylor University, 1956; First draft choice of Detroit Lions, 1957; Played for Lions 1958-61; Standout defensive player for Cleveland Browns during 1962 and 1963. Home: Corpus Christi, Texas*

THE GIANT FOOTBALL GUARD towered over the slim ministerial student as they walked from class across the Baylor University campus.

"Bill, I believe you *can* be All-American," the shorter student insisted.

"But, Larry, I'm not that good," Bill Glass replied. "I'd like to be, though — not just for myself — but to show people that a Christian can be a top-notch athlete."

"Let's pray about it," Larry suggested.

A few moments later the two were closeted together in a dormitory room. "Lord, Bill wants to be a better football player for Your glory — even an All-American, if it could be Your will."

Big Bill Glass fervently added, "Lord, all my strength and ability comes from Thee. Help me to play my best, and I will use the honor for Your glory."

Day after day Larry Walker and Bill Glass prayed in this manner. As they prayed, Bill worked hard to improve his gridiron talents. Then things began to happen. In a game with California, Bill made 17 unaided tackles. Bill's tackling helped Baylor in the 'Gator Bowl in 1955 and in the Sugar Bowl in 1956 where the team collected a 13-7 win over Tennessee, the number two team in the nation. Not only did he win All-American honors in 1956, but the professional Detroit Lions made him their No. 1 draft choice for the 1957 season.

However, Bill chose to go with his line coach, Jack Russell, to the Saskatchewan Rough Riders in the Canadian Football League. A year later he transferred to Detroit.

Bill was a standout defensive player for Detroit from 1958-61. He lived up to the estimate of Sam Boyd, his coach at Baylor, who had said, "Bill's as strong as a bull and can move. He's smart and has all the desire."

While at Detroit, Bill was given the job of stopping 275-pound, All-Pro Jim Parker, when the Lions played the Baltimore Colts. Parker, an offensive left tackle, had a reputation for taking care of would be tacklers. And Big Jim stood between Bill and the Colts' quarterback, Johnny Unitas. Again and again, Bill, weighing 255 pounds himself, was "taken care of" by Big Jim. Bill decided that "Parker must have a weakness somewhere."

Bill poured over films of Big Jim in action. The next time the Lions and the Colts met, Bill was ready.

When the ball was snapped, Bill charged toward Parker, Big Jim moved up, believing Bill would make contact with his hands and try to push through to the quarterback. But this time Bill zeroed into Big Jim head on, pitching him off balance with a hard shoulder blow. Parker reeled to one side and Bill charged on to nail the quarterback.

The Cleveland Browns secured Bill's services in a 1962 trade. Coach Paul Brown of the Cleveland club had once coached a squad in the Senior Bowl and remembered Bill as a player who "gave all he had." During 1962 and 1963 Bill, playing right defensive end for the Browns, has been a prime factor in the Cleveland team becoming contenders for the

National Football League championship. So great has been his pressure on the passer, that often two men are now assigned to stop him.

Bill is also one of the most popular players on the Cleveland squad. For two successive years he has spoken to the local "Touchdown Club," an organization of several hundred leading businessmen who root for the Browns. When Bill spoke to the club at their annual banquet last November, he showed that success had not made him forget the vow he had made when praying with Larry Walker.

"What's the solution to our world's problems?" Bill asked the businessmen. "Everywhere you hear the tramp, tramp, tramp of the revolutionaries. Here in America, divorce, crime and dope addiction are all on the increase. Last week a psychopathic killer murdered the president. What can we do about all this?

"Some have tried to find the answer through philosophy," Bill continued. "But philosophy is changeable and what was true yesterday may not be true today. Others say the whole meaning of life is nothingness, so they lead sloppy lives, not caring about the consequences.

"I've found the secret of purposeful living in Jesus Christ. With Him, I've been able to hit the issues of life head on.

"If a big guard moves toward me as I'm heading for his ball carrier, I must take care of the guard to get to the ball carrier. I cannot sidestep him, just as I cannot sidestep the real issues of life."

Then gesturing with a huge hand, Big Bill said intently, "When the crisis time comes all the philosophies of life will fail, but Jesus Christ will never fail. Death is certain. Three of our players died recently; Ernie Davis with leukemia, Don Fleming by electrocution and Tom Bloom in an auto accident. Now President Kennedy has been cut down by an assassin's bullet. I may die tomorrow, but if I do, I'm prepared — with Christ.

"But suppose I don't die. Suppose I'm injured and cannot

play football anymore. My purpose in living will not end then. I have Christ."

Bill's speech to the "Touchdown Club," coming just after the murder of President Kennedy, made a telling effect upon the businessmen. They were a sober, somber group as they filed out of the banquet hall.

Bill's influence on his teammates also shows evidence that he has not forgotten his main purpose in life. Several Brown players have come to Bill asking spiritual help and inquiring about his personal faith. To each, Bill has given his personal testimony, then said, "I've found the Christian life to be life at its best."

Off the field, Bill is frequently confronted by people who wonder how he finds football compatible with his Christian faith.

"Football is a way of life," Bill answers. "For me, it's a job I enjoy doing. It is competitve, and we play according to clearly defined rules. It demands a strong body, disciplined mind and hard work to achieve success. But most of all, football for me is a way to witness for Christ. I think I am a *better* football player because of the motivation Christ gives me."

On the field, Bill practices what he preaches. Once he fell on a ball-carrier a split second after the whistle blew. "I'm sorry," he apologized, "I just couldn't stop." Another time, a big lineman came across smashing at Bill with his fists. "He tried to rearrange the way I ate," Bill says. "It took more than self-control not to hit him back."

While a hard, jarring tackle does not affect his temper, Bill admits that a player who breaks the rules does get his goat. But here Bill's only rejoinder is to remind the rule-breaker, "you're not a very good football player if you have to play illegally."

Football is only part of Bill's life. The year round he averages speaking in one high school assembly each week. During the off-season he leads revivals in Baptist churches. He has been so effective that he is now booked solid for two years ahead. And recently Bill and five other Christian athletes made a film called, "Play for Keeps."

The film features, besides Bill Glass, five other outstanding Christian athletes: Felipe Alou, Raymond Berry, Bobby Richardson, Bill Wade and Alvin Dark. It features these five athletes in actual sports action and in giving their Christian witness.

To better prepare himself for "lay preaching," Bill has completed a full three-year theology course at Southwestern Baptist Theological Seminary in Fort Worth, Texas. Bill did the work in six consecutive off-seasons. "I don't think I should be ordained — at least, not now," Bill says. "As a layman and as a pro-football player, I can reach people a minister cannot reach. Kids in high school assemblies, in churches, outside the churches will listen to me because I have a 'name' in football."

A few days before the interview for this story, Bill spoke and showed the film, "Play for Keeps," in a Toledo, Ohio, church. Thirty young people came forward to commit themselves to Christ. Several were high school football players from a team that had come to hear Bill. In another of Bill's meetings, a football coach came forward to accept Christ.

Many times Bill cannot give an invitation to accept Christ. But even without the invitation, there's plenty of reaction afterward. An illustration is the English teacher who wrote Bill to thank him for speaking to her students. "You held their attention and inspired them so much," she said. "One of the more skeptical students told me, 'I've never heard anyone like that before. He believed what he said.'" Then the teacher added, "The thought has hit me rather forcefully since your visit that these rather sophisticated youngsters are more spiritually hungry than we know."

When conducting a revival, Bill takes time out to play touch football or some other active game with the boys. He asks the Christian boys to bring along their non-Christian friends to watch the demonstration. "This gives the Christian boys a chance to help win their friends," Bill says. "Playing with the boys gives me a chance to *show* them what Christ means to me."

Bill has a deep concern for teen-agers. He was 16 when he became a Christian.

"I joined the church at 10," Bill recalls, "but I didn't really have an experience with Christ. For the next six years, I was only a once-in-awhile attender. Then my dad got right with the Lord and the change in his life really shook me. My brother had been an All-State football star — he's now head coach at Lamar State Teachers College in Beaumont, Texas — and I thought the greatest goal in life was to become a star athlete. But then, I realized this was not the ultimate and I accepted Christ under the preaching of Dr. Warren Walker at the Second Baptist Church in Corpus Christi." Dr. Walker encouraged Bill to tell other boys about his new-found faith. Soon Bill was teaching a Sunday school class of boys.

Bill was not a standout player in high school until his senior year. "I had not matured physically," he says. "My feet and hands were big — I wore size 14 shoes. I had two 'left feet' and two 'left hands,' but I had the desire to play."

From several scholarships offered, Bill selected Baylor, a Baptist School at Waco, Texas. "I felt I needed the Christian training which a church school offers," Bill says.

At Baylor, Bill met Larry Walker who is now a pastor. The two became close friends and frequently prayed together. Today Bill credits Larry with "making me believe I could be an All-American and an outstanding football player."

There was another Baylor student who was destined to have a potent influence upon Bill's life. But Mavis Knapp didn't enroll until Bill was a senior and a star football player.

Mavis, 5'4" with dark hair, was a "living doll" in the eyes of some of the Baylor boys. But she confided to her Sunday school teacher that "I'm disappointed at the way some so-called Christian boys act on dates."

"There's one boy who lives what he preaches," the teacher said proudly. "He teaches a large freshmen college boys class in our church. He gets his boys out of bed on Sunday morning and sees to it they're in Sunday school on time."

Mavis' dark eyes flashed with admiration. "What's his name?"

"Bill Glass, and he plays football, too," the teacher added admiringly.

When Mavis returned to her room in the freshman dorm, she found a football program. She cut out Bill's picture and pasted it on her mirror. Several girls came in and noticed the picture. Mavis giggled as she said, "I'm going to get a date with him."

"Silly," one of the girls said, laughing. "He's a senior and they say he'll be All-American this year. You're only a freshman. Do you know him?"

"Not yet." Mavis tossed her curls jauntily.

"That'll be the day," one of the girls jibed in plain unbelief.

The news got around to Bill that Mavis wanted to meet him. Bill laughed her off as "just another silly freshman."

Despite the teasing of her skeptical girl friends, Mavis wrote to her folks. "I haven't met Bill yet, but I'm praying about him. I have the funniest feeling that if I ever meet him, it'll turn out to be real important."

Mavis regularly attended "Noonspiration," held just after lunch each day. One day when the program was finished, a boy she knew, asked, "Would you like to meet someone?"

Mavis turned around and there towering a foot over her stood Bill Glass. "He was standing there *soooo* big and laughing fit to kill," she said later. "I blushed all colors, said 'Hi,' and walked away."

But this wasn't the end. The following day at "Noonspiration," Mavis met Bill again.

"I'm preaching at a church near here next Sunday," he said casually. "I need a piano player."

"I can't play the piano," Mavis said weakly.

"Then, maybe you can sing."

"I can't sing, either." Mavis hung her head, then added, "but I can play the harmonica."

"Really?" Bill said.

"I was just kidding. But I'd like to go anyway."

Bill shrugged his huge shoulders. "Okay, you can come and hear me preach."

When Bill came by to pick Mavis up at the dorm, her girl friends could hardly believe it. They crowded the windows, giggling and shouting tips to Mavis.

After church Bill took Mavis to a cafeteria. Mavis, a country girl, had never eaten in one before. "I took everything I saw," she said later. "Afterward, Bill told me, 'You eat more than any girl I ever took out.'"

After Bill returned her to the dorm, Mavis cried, thinking Bill did not like her. But being elected a homecoming representative by a campus club gave her the chance to ask Bill to be her escort for the homecoming game.

From then on, Bill took the offensive. Several dates later, Bill inquired if Mavis would like to sign a contract with him for life. The following year they were married and have lived happily ever since.

Big Bill and tiny Mavis now have three little Glasses, Billy 6, Bobby 4 and Mindy 1, who is not much larger than a regulation football.

Little Bill wants to be an astronaut "so I can jump as high as daddy." Football's too rough, he thinks, although he enjoys watching Bill make tackles on television. Bob, though, would like to be a football player when he grows up — "a Brown," he says.

Naturally they look on their football playing daddy as a V.I.P. Once when they were living in Fort Worth and Bill was attending the Baptist Seminary, little Bobby wandered into a neighbor's yard and began playing in a forbidden hole.

"You can't play there," the neighbor said. "I'm going to plant a tree."

Little Bobby stepped out of the hole and glared at the spoiler. "Do you know who my daddy is?"

The man knew well enough, but he decided to play along with the boy.

"And, who is your daddy, young man?"

"My daddy is Bill Glass! That's who!"

"And what's so important about Bill Glass?" the neighbor continued with a sly twinkle in his eye.

"He's a Christian!"

The neighbor was caught off guard by the four-year-old's reply. All he could think of was, "Then you be a good little Christian and get out of that hole."

# 11

## JERRY KINDALL

Second Baseman With the
Solutions to Life's Problems

**Second Baseman: Minnesota Twins**
*All-American baseball player at the
University of Minnesota, 1956; Chicago Cubs bonus player.*
*Home: Minneapolis, Minnesota*

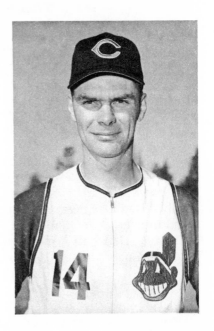

WE HAD JUST SWEPT a four-game series with the Yankees. I had eight hits in my first nine times at bat in the series and had won the second game with a homer in the ninth inning. The sweep put our Cleveland club in first place for the league pennant. Believe me, I was feeling great.

"But the next day we played the Boston Red Sox and I was shut out without a hit in five times at bat. To make matters worse, the Sox got the winning run off my fielding error.

"Yet that's baseball for you. It's an up and down game. A player can go from the hero to the goat within a few hours. One day the fans will be screaming their delight; the next day they will be howling their disapproval. But the stabilizing power of God's Spirit living within me has helped me cope with ups and downs."

So says Jerry Kindall, former All-American baseball player at the University of Minnesota and now a second baseman for the Cleveland Indians. Never a colorful .300 hitter in the majors, Jerry has gone unnoticed by many baseball fans.

But not by the fans in Cleveland. The *Cleveland Plain Dealer* has called Jerry the "best fielding second baseman since Joe Gordon." And last April 23, Cleveland's Wahoo Club gave Jerry the Golden Tomahawk award as "the most underrated Indian player of 1962."

But Jerry was never underrated by his father, whom he credits with being a major influence in preparing him to be a champion athlete. The Kindall home in St. Paul, Minnesota, was unpretentious. The family budget was slim. Jerry's father had to work at two jobs to support the family and pay medical expenses for Jerry's invalid mother. But Jerry recalls gratefully, "Dad was never too busy to play baseball with his boys and to take us to church and Sunday school at Elim Covenant Church. Dad had grown up during the depression and had taken a man's job at 16. He loved athletics and he wanted us to have the chance he didn't have."

Jerry's first play toy was a rubber bat and ball and when he was older he and his brother, Wayne, got in plenty of hitting and sliding practice in the Kindall backyard. When the family budget wouldn't permit buying a bat, Jerry's father solved the problem by bringing home worn out switchman's clubs from the railroad yard where he worked as a clerk.

When Jerry was 12 the family moved to a new house. Mr. Kindall sodded the yard with new grass. But the temptation was too great for Jerry and Wayne. One afternoon Mr. Kindall came home from the railroad yard to find a big bare spot in his new back lawn. The culprits quickly confessed. They needed sliding practice and the grass wasn't as tough as they expected. "No excuse," the big Swedish railroad man said. "Bend over and take your medicine." To this day Jerry still remembers the hard spanking. And the bald spot on the Kindall's back lawn is still there.

In high school Jerry battled fiercely to become a champion in sports. He earned four letters in baseball — playing shortstop — and three letters in basketball — playing center. His Washington High School team was city champs three times and Minnesota state champions once. His basketball team won the city title twice.

Jerry eagerly digested the sports pages, memorized the batting averages of his favorite baseball players, and dreamed of the day when he would play in the major leagues.

During high school Jerry was a model in behavior. He neither smoked, cursed or drank. He made excellent grades. He went to church and Sunday school regularly and frequently led devotions in youth fellowship at Elim Covenant Church. He was due to receive an athletic scholarship at the University of Minnesota. Yet, he declares today, "There was something lacking — a full commitment to Christ as Lord of my life.

"I joined the church at about 11," Jerry recalls, "but in my Christian life I only went through the motions and gave lip service to Christ. The Christian life for me was a frustrating experience.

"Then I started attending a Young Life club meeting in high school. Slowly I became aware of the difference between my brand of nominal Christianity and the all-out committed life for Jesus Christ.

"The climax for me came at a Young Life camp in Colorado Springs, Colorado, which I attended with Bruce Sundburg, a fellow student. Bruce showed me that the Christian life could be real joy and adventure. I noticed that Bruce got a bigger bang out of sports than I did. His life didn't rise or fall with sports as mine did. He had — through his faith — a steady rein on the problems of his life.

"As we memorized our Navigators' Scripture verses together, the Lord began speaking to my heart. I became aware that God wanted more from me than church attendance and lip service. He wanted to be first in my life, even ahead of baseball.

"My life began to take on real zest and joy. My nagging worry about life after death was eased. My uncertain future became certain with Christ as my Guide. My goal to go to college and develop into a major league ball player moved into the background. Matthew 6:33 — 'Seek ye first the kingdom of God and his righteousness, and all these things shall be added unto you' — became meaningful.

"My life didn't take on a new behavior pattern. I had

outwardly lived a Christian life before. But I came to know that being in Christ means to allow self to dwell within Christ's will and love. I committed myself to follow Christ one step at a time and leave my future with Him."

God's future for Jerry included a basketball scholarship at the University of Minnesota. But he stood out in baseball. In his junior year he batted .440, won All-American honors, and his team won the National Collegiate title in Omaha, Nebraska. In the semi-final game against the University of Mississippi Jerry smashed a home run, a triple, a double and a single in four times at bat.

God's future for Jerry also included Georgia Nelson, a dark-haired student nurse whom Jerry came to know at Inter-Varsity Christian Fellowship meetings. For their first date they attended a campus production of the play, "Annie, Get Your Gun." A year and a half later Jerry got his girl. Today Jerry and Georgia have a daughter, Betsy 6, and two future young boy athletes, Douglas 4 and Bruce 2.

Jerry was tapped for the major leagues during his junior year of college. Seven clubs offered him contracts. But before he could decide which contract to sign, he had to settle a personal question: Could he, a Christian, play professional baseball on Sunday?

"This was one of the toughest problems I ever faced in my Christian life," Jerry says today. "I felt I had to face it *before* I signed a contract."

What factors influenced Jerry to believe that he could in good conscience play baseball on Sunday?

"First," Jerry says, "I prayed about the matter and became convinced that God had given me the ability and opportunity to be an ambassador for Him in the major leagues, and baseball players *must* play on Sunday. Now after eight years in professional baseball I feel this more strongly than when I first signed.

"But," Jerry adds, "if my baseball career should ever keep me from regularly worshiping with other Christians on Sunday, then I would get out. I feel that we should 'not forsake the assembling of ourselves together' (Hebrews 10:25). Playing baseball on Sunday does not keep me from church. I can go to a morning service if we are playing a Sunday night game or to an evening service if we are playing an afternoon game."

Having settled the Sunday playing question, Jerry turned his attention to selecting one of the clubs which had offered him a contract. He finally chose the Chicago Cubs and joined the team as a bonus player on July 1, 1956. Chicago was close to home (Minneapolis did not have a major league club at that time) and he had always been a Cub fan.

Jerry's first year in the majors was a disappointment to him. From batting .440 in college he skidded to .164. "I was over my head playing with experienced players," Jerry explains. "The stability I had in Christ helped me not to become a washout. It was also a lesson in humility."

After a year and a half with the Cubs, Jerry was sent to the Fort Worth Cats, a minor league club, to learn to play second base. That year the Fort Worth Club won the pennant in the Texas League, and Jerry was named to the All-Star team. In 1959 Fort Worth moved up to the American Association. Jerry had another good year and the team went to the finals of the American Association playoff.

"I gained plenty of good experience playing in the minors," Jerry says today. "I also gained some spiritual victories."

One of Jerry's "spiritual wins" came in 1958 when he fell into a bad batting slump and struck out two games in a row. "Before, I had brushed off my down-in-the-dumps feelings as being 'natural,'" Jerry recalls. "But suddenly I realized that I had reserved a little island of self-pity. I surrendered this to Christ and discovered that in His strength I could rejoice even in a batting slump. I reasoned that His power in my life did not have to fizzle just because of my failure to hit a baseball.

"After this many players told me, 'I've been looking for you to blow up after a slump, but you remained calm and even seemed happy. How do you do it?' Each time provided an opportunity to tell another player about Christ."

In 1960 Jerry was called back by the Cubs. That year he played second base and hit .242. The following year he played second base and shortstop and hit .240. In November of 1961 he was traded to the Cleveland Indians, the club he played for until June, 1964. Here he proved to be a sharp fielder and a solid booster of team spirit. No one has ever accused Jerry of being a "complainer." At the opening of the 1963 season, he was not "started" at second base. Woodie Held took his place. Jerry told a sports writer, "I want to play but I hold no hard feelings. Woodie is a fine ball player."

Like other Christian athletes, Jerry gives much of his off-season time for speaking to church groups and helping as a Young Life leader in Minneapolis. Jerry and Georgia are currently members of First Covenant Church in Minneapolis where Jerry teaches senior highs in the Sunday school.

Also, like other Christian athletes, Jerry finds plenty of illustrations in sports that apply to the Christian life. Frequently he talks about commitment. "We go out on the field to win a baseball game," he says. "Every play that we make is pointed at this goal. We must do the same in the game of life. We must commit our emotions, ambitions and wills to Christ. We must allow Him to take over. Only then will we succeed."

Sometimes Jerry uses contrasts. "In baseball you find the Mickey Mantles and the average guys; the major leagues and the minor leagues," he says. "But the greatest contrast is in the lives of people — between those who are surrendered to Christ and those who are not.

"Playing baseball requires discipline. I must practice, keep my body in shape, eat the right foods and go to bed at the right times. Likewise in the Christian life there are certain habits and amusements that are wrong for me. My body is the temple of the Holy Spirit. Whatever defiles the residence of the Holy Spirit is wrong for me."

Those who know Jerry best say that he is a good speaker. But more important, they say, is the life he lives both on and off the field. Fellow Christian athletes call Jerry a "deep" Christian whose faith shows up at home.

Jerry and Georgia regularly invite other athletes and their families into their home. "We enjoy their company," Jerry says, "and we have the chance to give a Christian witness."

When Jerry was playing in Fort Worth, they invited a young pitcher to dinner. Afterward, they asked if he would like to sit in on their family devotions. He did and was deeply impressed. Later he said to Jerry, "I'm getting married in a few weeks. How can I have a Christian home like yours?"

"Before you can have a Christian home, you must have Christian people in the home," Jerry replied. Then he explained how to become a Christian. A few days later on a plane flying from Minneapolis to Denver, the young pitcher trusted Christ.

Like other athletes, Jerry knows that his occupation will not always be professional baseball. He isn't worried. "My life is joined to the great mainstream of God's purpose," he says.

"I'm working on a Master's degree in physical education at the University of Minnesota. I have my B.S. degree in English Literature. I am preparing to teach or coach or do both. Perhaps I will go into full-time Christian work. But all of this will be worked out in God's great purpose for my life."

Jerry's favorite author is the old master, William Shakespeare. Why? "Shakespeare has a deep insight into human problems," Jerry says. "His characters are true to life. They are human beings in need . . . searching for reality. Unfortunately, the brilliant Shakespeare does not give the answer to his characters' needs. I see a comparison here with modern novels. Today's novelists deal with sin but few present God's answer. I have found that answer in the Bible. For me, Christ meets the deepest needs of my personality. He has become the supreme *find* in my quest for the meaning of life."

(In June, 1964, Jerry went to the Minnesota Twins where he is expected to boost their infield strength.)

# 12

## JIM RAY SMITH

The Lineman Who Lays It
on the Line

**Offensive Guard: Dallas Cowboys**
*All-American, Baylor, 1953; Baylor team captain, 1954; All-Pro Guard in 1959, '60, '61, '62. Pro-Bowl Player, 1959, '60, '61, '62.*
*Home: West Columbia, Texas*

NO ONE WAS SURPRISED when Jim Ray Smith was named to the all-time Cleveland Browns pro-football team three years ago. Jim Ray is the kind of Texan whom Western badmen would even fear to tackle.

Jim Ray is big and powerful — 6′ 3″, 245 pounds — like a grizzly, but fast as a deer. When playing for the Browns, he was fast enough to keep ahead of fullback Jim Brown's smashing drives, while throwing some of the smoothest blocks in football. Now a mainstay for the Dallas Cowboys, Jim Ray is continuing to throw the kind of blocks that has earned him "All-Pro" honors during the last four years.

Off the gridiron, Jim Ray is a soft-spoken real estate man who teaches Sunday school and gives out pictures of himself autographed with a verse from the Bible. Hearing his gentle drawl, you find it easy to forget that he's a hard-charging, bone-jarring professional guard who meets head on the toughest of tacklers. But when you look at his record, you discover why he's one of the most respected guards in pro-ranks today.

Jim Ray was a four sports star at West Columbia, Texas,

High School who excelled in football, and was chosen to play in the Texas High School All-Star football game in 1951. "It was the biggest thrill of my life," says Jim Ray.

Baylor liked the way he moved tacklers around in the All-Star game and signed him to a scholarship. Bear fans were glad, because Jim Ray made All-Southwest Conference during 1953 and 1954. Jim put the icing on the cake when his two extra-point kicks and outstanding blocking and tackling brought Baylor to an upset win over previously undefeated Texas A & M. This earned him the honor of "Associated Press Lineman of the Week." In 1953 a team of football coaches named Jim Ray to *Collier* magazine's All-America team. The following year Jim Ray captained the Baylor gridders. Then in the summer of 1955 he helped the College All-Stars squeeze out the National Football League's Champion Cleveland Browns — a 30-27 victory. However, long before the All-Star game the Browns had the rangy Texan pegged as their No. 7 draft choice.

Jim Ray didn't report to the Browns until 1956, after he had served a stretch in the Army. After a year at defensive end, Coach Paul Brown switched Jim Ray to offensive guard just before the 1957 season got under way. Here he helped clear the way for Jim Brown and Bobby Mitchell to become big ground gainers with the Browns. With his classic blocking and genius for keeping would-be tacklers out of play, Jim Ray easily became a coach's dream lineman. "Everything a guard can do, Smith can do better," said one coach. For four successive seasons — 1959, '60, '61, '62 — Jim Ray was selected to play in the National Football League All-Star game (the Pro Bowl).

One of Jim Ray's first chores in Cleveland was to find a good church. He and his wife, Paula, attended the Cedar Hill Baptist Church because "the pastor preached the Gospel and the people didn't 'ooh' or 'ahh' over football players." The Smiths became good friends of the choir director, Bob Milner, even though they didn't sing in the choir. And it wasn't long until the choir man asked Jim Ray and another pro-footballer,

Pete Brewster, to tell about their Christian faith in a church brotherhood meeting.

Jim Ray who has no qualms about meeting 300 pound muscle-men on the football field, quaked from head to toe when he got up to speak. "It was the roughest assignment I ever had," he recalls. "Anybody could tell I was nervous. I stammered something about how God has a plan for each of us and that He will lead us if we'll let His will be our will. Then I told briefly about how I had become a Christian."

Today Jim Ray is no longer shy about speaking. He frequently talks to church groups about Christianity and athletics. "I committed my life to Christ when I was 13," he recalls, "but I was too timid to join the church then. My pastor back in West Columbia, Texas, declared that believing and trusting in Christ is the only way to heaven. That night I knelt by my bed and asked the Lord to forgive my sins and to come into my heart. And I promised that whatever I became — doctor, lawyer, ditch digger — I would do it to the glory of God. But not until after I was married and in the Army did I join a church and fully dedicate my life to Christ. Paula had a lot to do with that."

Jim Ray met Paula Braden at Baylor. He spotted the brown-eyed brunette from Dallas when she was moving into the girl's dormitory as a freshman. He introduced himself, but by the time he had gotten around to call her for a date, he had forgotten her name. Fortunately his roommate had a better memory.

"I was a senior then," Jim Ray says, "and had been slipping in my Christian convictions. I had been running with the wrong crowd and had begun taking an occasional drink. Paula challenged me to get back on the right track."

A few weeks after his first date with Paula, Jim Ray was inducted into the Army. On his first furlough they were married. Paula joined Jim Ray at camp in Fayettville, North Carolina. Here Jim Ray joined a Baptist church, dedicating his home and future to the Lord. Today Paula and Jim Ray have two future rookies of their own; James Ray II, 6 and Brad, 3.

Frequently Jim Ray is asked, "How can you as a Christian participate in the rough game of professional football?" The big Texan sets his jaw firmly and says, "Football may be a bit rough, but most guys play clean. There are very few fights, and some of these are blown up by the press. I've been injured a few times — that's part of the game — but I can remember having only one run-in with a player. That was when Big Daddy Lipscomb lost his temper and kicked me. I got a little mad, but it was all over in a few minutes.

"The Lord gave me the ability and I feel He has opened the door for me to play. For me it's a way to witness for Christ, not only to the fans and hero-worshiping kids, but to teammates also."

How does a player witness to his teammates? "You never put the rush on these guys," Jim Ray says. "If you live what you profess, they'll not only respect you, but some will come asking for spiritual help. And by living the Christian life before the guys, I don't mean cramming it down their throats. When I came to the Browns some of the boys invited me to a party. There was a lot of drinking and carousing going on and I told them, 'This isn't my kind of life.'"

Jim can recount many opportunities he has had to share his Christian faith with players who were curious to know more about his "brand of religion."

One day in training camp, a husky lineman came to him. "I understand you're religious and believe in prayer and that sort of stuff."

"Well, I don't know how religious I am," Jim Ray drawled back. "But I'm a Christian, if that's what you mean. Something I can help you with, pardner?"

"The coach and I have had a disagreement," the player said seriously. "He thinks I'm not ready for the first squad. I think I am. Do you think if I pray that God will change the coach's mind?"

"I really don't know," Jim Ray replied. "I figure a guy must be a Christian before the Lord will answer his prayer."

"Religion isn't my best talent," the lineman said.

"Say," Jim Ray suggested, "we're having a Bible study

over at Bill Glass' apartment. Would you like to join us?
Might help you to know how to pray."

The inquirer eagerly nodded his head. "Sure. Count me
in."

A few evenings later Jim Ray, Bill Glass and Jim Shofner,
another Christian player, huddled with the concerned lineman. With the New Testament as their rule book they showed
him how to become a Christian. Before the session had broken
up, the player had accepted Christ.

"Thanks, fellows," he told them when leaving. "I've been
plenty mixed up. But you showed me the way tonight."

Remembering that experience, Jim Ray says, "It's great
to have the honor of playing pro-ball before a packed stadium
of fans, but helping somebody come to Christ is a greater
honor. In pro-football another player soon takes your place
and you're forgotten. But honor with Christ remains forever.

"Millions of people are looking today for kicks, thrills,
happiness — call it what you will," Jim Ray adds. "The fans
that pack the stands to watch us play come thinking they will
get more out of life by watching a football game. Now I think
it's fine to watch football games — even better to play. But
the real purpose and meaning in life are only found in Christ.

"I know a player who goes to different churches looking
for what he calls truth. He's dabbled with several types of
businesses during the off-season. But he refuses to face the
real issue of life: whether to accept Christ and eternal life or
to continue on the way he's going — to eternal death.

"This guy could learn a lesson from the game he plays.
In football we're always moving toward the goal. Our purpose is to make a touchdown. We don't waste our time running around in circles."

Jim Ray has been in the game of football for a third of
his life. He finds many other comparisons between the game
of football and the game of life.

"In football every game is crucial," he says. "There's
always the challenge to win. A football player must be consistent, dedicated to his job. I'm a lineman. My job isn't to
run with the ball, but to keep the opposing lineman from

tackling the man who is going for yardage. I don't make the headlines like the ball carriers do. But guys like me are necessary. If we miss our blocks, then the ball carrier doesn't get through. I guess you could call me a lineman in my church. I'm not a preacher or a music director. But I give my money and help in Sunday school. The preacher couldn't get along without linemen like me in the pews backing him up.

"In football the line is no better than its weakest man. Every man has to hold up his end. You can't run from a tackler who gives you a rough time. You have to grit your teeth and hit him head on. This takes courage. A lot of guys can't take it and burn out. It's like this in the church. Here's the preacher running with the ball — preaching the Gospel. When the linemen — laymen — are strong, the opponent can't break through and throw them for a loss. But when somebody gives in to the tempter, the preacher and his message are discredited. How many times have I heard a guy say, 'I would be a Christian except for a certain church member I know.'

"Pro-football players, like everybody else, meet a lot of temptation. We travel a lot and are given big parties — sometimes by breweries who want to cash in on our names. A Christian athlete has to keep his guard up at all times. He can overcome if he'll let the Lord help him. 'There hath no temptation taken you but such as is common to man: but God is faithful, who will not suffer you to be tempted above that ye are able; but will with the temptation also make a way to escape, that ye may be able to bear it' (I Corinthians 10:13).

"Fighting temptation is like playing the first quarter of a football game. If you can hold your slot in the line for the first quarter, you'll gain self-confidence and your opponents will respect you for the rest of the game. Every good block makes you stronger for the next one. And in life, overcoming the temptation makes you stronger to face the tempter the next time.

"A football player gives and takes lots of hard knocks. You have to learn to take the losses with the wins. But reverses are good for athletes, just as they're good for Christians. It's the little setbacks that discipline and temper me. I get on my feet, dig in and hit the opponent harder next time. Then when a big loss comes, I can take it without being chased off the field.

"Right after I came into pro-football I had what I thought was a big set-back. An injured shoulder started giving me trouble. The coach gave me two weeks of rest. Then I went back in and pulled a muscle. The coach called me a 'softie,' an 'easy touch,' and a few other things that are unprintable. He ended by saying, 'Looks as if we'll have to get rid of you.'

"I called Paula in Dallas and told her I'd probably be coming home. Then I went to my room and packed. *This is the end of pro-football for me,* I told myself. But before checking out I knelt and poured out my bitterness in prayer. As I asked God for guidance, a voice seemed to whisper, 'Try another week.'

"Then I remembered. The coach hadn't actually dropped me from the team. He had simply ridiculed me — bawled me out — hurt my pride. I went back on the field and the coach moved me to a new position where my injured shoulder didn't get so much punishment. I played the rest of the year and have been in pro-ball ever since."

Besides his football career, Jim Ray operates a successful commercial real estate business in Dallas. In business, as in football, Jim Ray uses opportunities to tell others about Christ.

Recently, one Tuesday morning, Jim Ray and Paula were having morning devotions. "Lord, lead us to someone today who needs to know about You," Jim Ray prayed. A few hours later, Jim called on a businessman client. When the client's secretary greeted Jim Ray, she said, "I hear that you're quite religious."

And that was the big Texan's cue to say, "I don't know how religious I am, but I do know I'm a Christian. Are you?"

Solemnly she shook her head.

"Would you like to know how to become a Christian?"

She nodded her head.

So Jim Ray told her and when he left she knew.

# 13

## DAVE WICKERSHAM

The Apple Pitcher Who Made
the Big League

**Pitcher: Detroit Tigers**
*Won 11 out of 15 games pitched
in 1962 for Kansas City Athletics;
Pitched shutout against New York
Yankees on July 29, 1963.*
*Home: East Springfield, Pennsylvania*

Look, Davey, this is the way you catch the ball. Turn your
fingers down and let the ball roll in."

The older boy walked across the room and plopped down
beside the wall. "Now catch it, Davey." He rolled the red
rubber ball across the floor. "Atta boy, Davey, you'll be a
major leaguer yet."

Dave Wickersham was too young then to know what the
major leagues meant. But he liked to play roll-the-ball with
his older cousin.

Soon Davey was old enough to join the pickers in his
father's apple orchard. One day when his father wasn't looking . . . .

"Pssst, Davey. Can you hit the basket?"

Six-year-old Davey fired a plump red apple at the basket
his cousin was holding.

"Whammo! Atta boy, Davey. Now hit it again."

Davey did hit it again and again and again. But his apple-
pitching skill soon got him into trouble.

99

"Hey, who hit me?" The apple picker looked around carefully. He saw a freckled face peering around a tree. "Hey, Mr. Wickersham, Davey's throwing apples at us again."

Forthwith came Davey's father. "All right, boy, your fun's over. Come and take your medicine."

"Aw, Dad, I was just building my pitching arm," Davey protested.

"I'm going to build up another part of your anatomy," his father replied, grinning. "C'mon, boy. It hurts me more than it hurts you."

When the switching was over, Davey wasn't so sure his father was right. But a few more switchings convinced him that it would be healthier to develop his arm in other ways.

Came high school days for Dave, and he was still pitching. Now his father was sitting in the stands cheering.

"Strike 'em out, Davey. Strike 'em out," the big Pennsylvania apple farmer yelled.

Davey struck 'em out so many times that soon after he graduated the Pittsburgh Pirates offered him a contract to play in their farm system.

Two years later — 1957 — the apple-pitching pitcher from West Springfield, Pa., led all the Big State (Texas) League. On the mound for Beaumont, Dave held batters to a 1.95 earned run average and earned League All-Star honors.

In 1959 he pitched Gastonia, North Carolina, to the Sally League playoff crown. In the playoff Dave received credit for three of Gastonia's six wins. In 19 innings of pitching he allowed only one earned run and won the final game with a three-hitter.

In November of 1959 he was drafted from the Pirates by the Kansas City Athletics. During the 1960 and 1961 seasons, Wickersham pitched for the A's farm club, Shreveport, and held his earned run averages down to 2.64 and 2.45. That was proof enough for the A's that the boy from the Pennsylvania apple orchard was ready for the big leagues.

On May 22, 1962, Dave pitched his first major-league game as a starter. He downed the Boston Red Sox 5-1, allowing only five hits. That year — his first year in the majors — Dave spent several weeks on the bench with an injury. But despite his injury he managed to compile 11 wins with only 4 losses. In 1963, Dave's record was not as good — 12 wins and 15 losses. But his teammates showed their estimate of him by electing him to represent the Athletics for the off-season meeting of players' representatives with league officials.

Dave's biggest major league win came on July 29, 1963. He was in New York pitching against the Yankees. "My roommate, Charley Poor, was on my mind all during the game," Dave recalls. "Charley's had polio since he was seven, and he was in Houston undergoing serious surgery while I was pitching. I prayed for Charley before the game. I prayed for myself as I always do before a game — 'Lord, help me to do my best. Help me to stay calm and not argue with the umpires.' Then I went out and pitched a 5-0 shutout. When the last man was out, I dedicated the game to Charley. Then when I heard his operation was a success, my day was complete. It was my biggest day in baseball — and my biggest thrill, except for the day when I became a Christian."

Dave was only 12 at the time and was attending the Lake Erie Bible Camp near Erie, Pa. The counselor happened to be Jack Augustine, son of Dave's pastor.

One day in their cabin, Jack asked Dave, "Are you sure that you are a Christian?"

Dave nervously shuffled his feet and looked down at the floor. "No, I'm not sure, and I wish I was," he blurted out. "Going to church and Sunday school all my life — well, I've thought things were okay. But now I know that I haven't got what some of the other kids here have."

Jack quietly took out his New Testament. "Read this verse," he said.

Dave looked at the verse and blinked, "I know that verse by heart."

"Just read it, Dave, and when you come to the word 'whosoever,' put your name there."

So Dave read, "For God so loved the world, that he gave his only begotten Son, that — if Dave Wickersham — believeth in him should not perish, but have everlasting life."

"What does it say to you, Dave?"

"God gave His only Son" — Dave paused — "so that I might have everlasting life."

"What do you have to do?"

Dave ran his finger carefully over each line of the verse. "Why, just believe, I guess."

Slowly the truth dawned. "Maybe before I didn't really think of it as meaning me," Dave said slowly.

"Believe means trust," Jack said. "Will you believe now —accept Christ, *now?*"

Dave spoke hesitatingly. "There's something bothering me, Jack. Do you think that I'd have to give up playing baseball, if I really believed in Jesus?"

Jack grinned and shook his head. "I know how much you love to play, Dave. No, I don't think so. But God wants you to love Him, even more than baseball."

"Let me read the verse again," Dave asked.

When he had finished, Jack asked, "Are you ready to believe — to accept Christ as your Savior?"

Dave nodded.

"Then let's tell Him about it."

Remembering that moment, Dave says, "I received real peace and assurance that has never left me. I left the camp with a wonderful feeling in my heart. I remember especially how happy I felt. I was a Yankee fan then and my team had just won 17 games in a row. The other guys at camp were rooting for the Pirates. I was happy about what the Yankees were doing, but when I accepted Christ into my heart — I can't explain it — I felt even happier."

A few years later when Dave was offered a professional baseball contract, he wondered about the problem of Sunday baseball. Could he play and hold up his Christian testimony? He prayed about the matter and finally decided, "If God has given me the ability to play, then I should sign a contract."

"I love the game," Dave adds. "I'm so thrilled to be able to make a living doing what I really love. And at the same time I can show kids that it isn't sissy to go to church and Sunday school.

"I feel a big responsibility to the young people who see my name in the papers and watch me pitch. Dozens of kids write me asking for my picture. I send each one a little snapshot with my favorite verse of Scripture, Colossians 3:17, written just under my signature. Not long ago a boy in Connecticut wrote back that the verse had gotten him interested in Bible study and he had accepted the Lord as his Savior.

"A Christian baseball player," Dave continues, "just can't be too careful about the example he sets both on and off the diamond. Once I saw a game film showing me arguing with the umpire. The way my lips were moving, I knew the fans probably thought I was cursing the ump. So right then and there I made a new resolution and asked the Lord to help me stay off the umpire's back. Now before every game I ask the Lord to help me hold my temper. But it isn't easy. There are about 125 pitches in a regular game. The game can ride on every one. There're some mighty tense moments, but when I think I get a bad call, I just grit my teeth and say, 'Lord, help me keep my big mouth shut!' "

When asked about spitballs and beanballs, Dave had this to say, "I've got a great spitball, but I won't throw it. It's illegal. I'll never throw a beanball either and intentionally try to conk the batter in the head. Sure, I'll crowd the batter at the plate if he leans in too close. This is all part of the game. Last year I hit a batter who leaned in too close. I felt plenty bad, but we knew it was all part of the game. Around the big leagues, I have noticed very little dirty pitching. We play hard and play to win, but most of us nix the dirty pitch or play. It doesn't win for your team in the long run."

Does Dave feel nervous just before going in to pitch a big game? "Sure, I do," he says. "But before every game I pray, 'Lord, let Thy will be done.' And if I lose the game, the world doesn't end for me. I figure that there'll be another day. Besides I belong to Christ and doing His will is more important than winning a game. Christ gives me a sense of inner control. I'll always be satisfied with my inner self as long as I'm honoring Him."

Dave laughs heartily about the idea of a big leaguer having to drink or smoke to be popular. "That's a bunch of baloney," he says frankly. "I know many, many top athletes who neither drink nor smoke."

When asked about athletes who are seen in advertisements or television commercials extolling the delights of certain brands of cigarettes, Dave says bluntly, "Those guys are paid to do that! The cigarette money boys have never asked me. I think they know my feelings. They went after Vernon Law, a good buddy of mine, when he was pitching for the Pirates. Vern told the guy that he didn't believe in it, but the guy kept insisting that there was nothing wrong in selling one's name for a thousand bucks. From what I understand, Vern almost had to throw the guy out of his room.

"Sometimes the other guys kid me in the locker room. "If I've just won a game, a guy may say, 'Good game you pitched, Wick. Whatcha say? Let's celebrate it with a drink.' But they're just kidding. They know I don't drink.

"Sometimes a new player will offer me a cigarette or a beer. He doesn't know my convictions, so I tell him politely, 'No, thanks. I don't smoke or drink.' I know he means well so I try not to offend.

"Once in a while a guy will curse in my hearing. But then he'll turn around and say, 'Excuse me, Wick. Didn't know you were around.' Or, he'll say, 'I forgot you were here.' Really, I think it's too bad that a fellow gets the idea he has to smoke, drink or curse to be popular."

Dave at 27 is still unmarried. Naturally his friends kid him a lot. But he says, "I'm sure the Lord has the right girl for me. That's what's important, marrying in the Lord's will."

In Kansas City, Dave shares an apartment with Charley Poor, the polio victim mentioned earlier in this article, and with Bill Krisher, former professional football player for the Dallas Texans and All-American at the University of Oklahoma.

Poor wants to be a Christian psychologist and is finishing the work on his doctorate. Krisher is Associate Director of the Fellowship of Christian Athletes. "We're hardly ever all home at the same time," Dave says, "but sometimes we're able to have our devotions together. Both Bill and Charley are great guys. Charley's been in a wheel chair since he was 14 or 15. He comes to all the games I pitch in Kansas City. He's a real competitor. Last year he went to New York and won fourth place in the National Table Tennis championship for wheelchair cases. He plays a tough game at ping pong even with me standing up. Sometimes I help Bill out at the Fellowship of Christian Athletes, and when our schedule permits we attend Sunday school and church together at the Broadway Baptist Church in Kansas City.

"Bill's a football enthusiast, being a former All-American and all that," Dave adds cheerfully, "but baseball's my game. I love to play. But my life won't end when my time is up in the leagues. Maybe I'll coach or teach or something, but whatever I do I'll be doing the Lord's will.

"And that's what really counts in life for me — doing the Lord's will."

(Dave Wickersham was traded to the Detroit Tigers for the 1964 season where he has become the strongest pitcher in the Tiger bullpen. In February he acquired a wife, Carol Sue, who helps him keep track of the batting habits of American League sluggers.)

# 14

## CLENDON THOMAS

The Defensive Back Who
Holds the Line

**Defensive Back: Pittsburgh Steelers**
*All-American and co-captain, University of Oklahoma, 1957; Led nation's major college scorers in 1956; Los Angeles Rams 1958-61; Led all Steeler defensive backs in 1962 with 7 pass interceptions.*
*Home: Oklahoma City, Oklahoma*

THERE'S NO PLACE in professional football for guys who are afraid of getting hurt. We play the game hard. It's hit or be hit — tackle or be tackled. You've got to be up for every play and meet your opponent headon."

This is Clendon Thomas speaking, a tall strong-muscled Oklahoman who plays defensive back for the Pittsburgh Steelers. Though he weighs only 190 and stands 6′ 2″, players 50 to 75 pounds heavier respect his hard, jarring tackles. They know that he was All-American on the University of Oklahoma squad that won 47 games in a row — an all-time college record, and that during his junior year he led the nation's major college scorers.

He's also a top golfer, licensed pilot, horseman and successful home builder in Oklahoma City. At 28, and a bachelor, Clendon looks like the type frequently seen in cigarette or beer advertisments, except that he considers both "vices which hurt the body and influence of an athlete." He unashamedly credits "the teachings and influence of my church with helping me decide when I was young not to smoke or drink — a decision I've never regretted."

Clendon's church is Foster Baptist in Oklahoma City. Here his parents faithfully *took* him to Sunday school. Here, when he was 12, he publicly declared his faith in Jesus Christ. "My pastor, Brother Norman, was the type of minister a boy could talk to," Clendon recalls. "He understood teens — didn't spend all his time telling us what we shouldn't do. I think that's important when working with young people. They resent being told over and over how bad they are. You don't win them because of what you are *against,* but because of what you are *for."*

Although Clendon was regular in Sunday school and church he admits to being "the shy type — the kind who sat on the back pew and listened.

"Until I was a freshman in college I was afraid to give a devotion or speak," Clendon says. "Then a pastor persuaded me to speak at a Sunday school dinner. I thought it would be a small class of a dozen or so members. But when I got to the restaurant, I found a *large* group of adults, including Governor Ray Garrett, waiting to hear me speak. I literally trembled as I stood up. I stumbled and stuttered through my talk. I must have mumbled a hundred 'uhs' and 'ahs.' But afterward the governor thanked me for my sincerity. Well, I was sincere in my testimony for Christ, but I was also scared. Since then, I've given my testimony many times, but I'd still rather face the toughest tackler in the league than speak in public."

While Clendon may be shy at public speaking, a glance at his football record shows that he has not been timid on the gridiron.

At the University of Oklahoma, this soft-spoken young man . . .

— Set a career rushing record for the Big Eight Conference, gaining 2,282 yards in 310 carries during three seasons of varsity play.

— Set school records for most touchdowns (36) and most points scored (216) in a career.

— Led the nation's major college scorers in 1956 with 18 touchdowns. In all he scored touchdowns in 24 of the 30 regular season games in which he played.

— During his three years at Oklahoma, the Sooners won 31 of 32 games, two national championships, three conference titles and two Orange Bowl games.

— Was named to the All-Big Seven team as a junior and the All-Big Eight team as a senior. Was the conference's leading punt returner as a sophomore and senior and finished fifth in pass receiving as a junior.

— Was picked as a senior on the first All-American team by United Press, the Football Coaches Association and *The Sporting News.*

— Finished tenth in the voting for the Heisman trophy — given annually to the nation's top college football player.

— Was the leading ball-carrier in the Orange Bowl game following his senior year as he picked up 89 yards in 14 carries in 48-21 win over Duke.

— Played in the Senior Bowl and the Hula Bowl and was a member of the College All-Star team that downed the National Football League Champion, the Detroit Lions, 35-19.

With this type of college record, Clendon was a natural for professional football. In 1958 he was the number two draft choice of the Los Angeles Rams. But ankle and rib injuries hampered his early pro career. In 1961 the Pittsburgh Steelers purchased Clendon for a defensive back position.

Clendon has shown evidence of his college greatness in playing for the Steelers. In the biggest Steeler win of 1962 he made a number of key pass interceptions against the New York Giants. During the 1962 season Clendon led the Steelers' defensive squad in pass interceptions, averaged 28 yards on kickoff returns, and was named to the second All-National Football League defensive team by United Press International.

In college, Clendon was frequently the ball carrier who made touchdowns. Now, in pro-football, he has been switched to a defensive slot. How does he feel about being out of the limelight?

"My job is to do my best wherever my coach assigns me,"

he says, "and he feels I can help the Steelers most in defense. Playing defense is more important than a lot of fans realize. The team with the most recovered fumbles and pass interceptions usually wins. When I come off the field at the end of a game, I know if I have had a good day, even if the fans do not applaud. The feeling of a job well done is reward enough for me.

"It's the same with being on the Lord's team. We can't all 'carry the ball.' Some of us have to hold the line. I'm that type of a man. Although I'm not a minister, I try to be a witness and example for Christ in pro-football. In church I can give and pray and stand behind those who lead the Christian team. I can 'follow the rules' — that's extremely important in football — and do my best for the Lord.

"The Bible is my rule book," Clendon declares. "From it I learn that I am a sinner and that Christ died for my sins. I learn how to live in daily fellowship with God and how to be victorious over the temptations of Satan.

"A football player *must* know the rule book, or he may ignorantly cause his entire team to be penalized. Likewise, a Christian by not knowing or not following the 'rules' of the Christian life can penalize the effectiveness of his church.

"As a defensive back, I can't afford to make a mistake in a football game. Often I'm the only man between the ball carrier and our goal line. If I don't bring him down, he may score and win the ball game. I must be on my toes every minute.

"It's that way in the Christian life. You simply can't afford to let your guard down. Being single and on the road a lot, I meet strong temptation. I could throw away my testimony and influence for Christ in a single evening. But I *can't*. No, I don't go around pointing the finger at guys who do things I don't believe in. You don't win people — especially professional athletes — by condemning their vices. But you can reach them by maintaining a steady Christian testimony. Not long ago a player said to me, 'Clendon, I admire you because you're strong enough not to drink.' I appreciated what he said — it confirmed again that a guy doesn't have to drink to be liked — but he was partly wrong. My strength comes from the Lord, not from myself."

Like many other Christian athletes, Clendon works with the Fellowship of Christian Athletes in presenting Christian programs to school assemblies. "Because of our 'names,' we can really sell Christianity," he says. "The kids simply don't expect to hear a professional athlete talk about his faith.

"Not long ago we presented a program in an Indiana high school located in a high delinquency area. Gary Demarest, a minister who works with the FCA, went along with us. The principal started off by 'eating the kids out' about the way they were acting. Then he introduced Gary as a minister. We could hear the groans as Gary got up to speak. The kids were expecting a pious 'be-good' lecture.

"But Gary did nothing but tell jokes for about 15 minutes. Then he introduced us. We knew the kids were expecting more of the same. But we jolted them by telling what Christ meant in our lives and how happy we were to be on His team. We told them that He was the reason why we lived clean lives. They received us with real respect. It's that way in every school where we present a program. The door is open for Christian athletes to speak. I'm sure I've been in some schools where a religious program has not been allowed in assembly for years — if ever."

Clendon admits that Sunday playing bothered him when he first entered professional football. "Then I checked up," he says, "and found that on one professional team only four out of 36 players were avowed Christians. I knew then that God had put me in professional football to be a witness for Christ.

"Really, we have no choice about playing on Sunday. It's either play or get out of the National Football League. I feel that God gave me the talent to play and that even on Sunday I can play for His glory.

"We pro-footballers are not the irreverent bunch that some people think we are," Clendon says with a broad grin. "Several Steelers are not ashamed to speak for Christ. During the season we hold our own Protestant worship service before the game of the day. About half of the guys on the squad attend. Most of the other fellows go to their Catholic mass."

What does the future hold for Clendon?

"I plan to go back to Oklahoma City and manage my home building business," he says. "I can serve the Lord as a Christian layman and be a witness to other businessmen."

And marriage?

"I'm looking," he says.

What kind of a girl is a top Christian athlete looking for?

"A Christian. One who holds the same convictions I do. One who loves me, not just because of my 'name,' but just for my own sake."

When he speaks about marriage, Clendon has stars in his eyes. But then why shouldn't he look for his idea of a "dream girl." In more ways than one, the handsome young Oklahoman is a "star," himself.

# 15

## BILL KRISHER

He Refused to Accept Defeat

**Associate Director: Fellowship of Christian Athletes**
*All-American guard, University of Oklahoma, 1956, '57; Played pro-football for Pittsburgh Steelers and Dallas Texans; Captain of Texans in 1960 and All-Pro Offensive Guard. Home: Midwest City, Oklahoma*

EVERY EYE WAS on the kicker as he ran toward the ball. If he made the extra point his team would tie Midwest City.

The Midwest City line rushed to meet him. The kicker's foot smacked leather, lifted the ball . . . but not far enough. Smashing in came Bill Krisher, a 160-pound fourteen-year-old tackle for Midwest City. Midwest fans roared. Their star tackle had blocked the kick. Moments later they won the game by the margin of one point.

Now it was 1957, seven years later. Bill Krisher (pronounced Crysher) was playing for the University of Oklahoma Sooners. For two seasons they had been undefeated in college play. They were playing the Colorado Buffaloes and running hard toward a third undefeated season. Late in the game Colorado scored a touchdown that brought the Buffaloes within one point of the Sooners. Colorado's place-kicking specialist came in to try for the extra point. If he should make it, Oklahoma's victory train would be halted. The college fans waited tensely. The Buffalo kicker moved forward. Then just as his toe touched the ball, Bill Krisher dived through the line to block the kick. Once again, Bill Krisher — now nicknamed the "Crusher" — had saved a crucial game. The Sooners rolled on to more victories, finally reaching a 47-game streak which was not broken until November 16, 1957, when Notre Dame took the Sooners by one touchdown.

Now it was 1958. Big Bill Krisher, weighing 240 pounds, crouched in the Pittsburgh Steeler line. This was pro-football where college men are separated from college boys.

A big tackle from the opposite team leered at Bill. "I've heard you're a Sunday school guy, 'Crusher.'" The guard paused, spat out a string of curses, then added, "I'm going to hit you so ——— hard you'll lose your religion."

The "Crusher" smiled back in reply and said nothing. The ball was snapped. The "Crusher" uncoiled and leaped at the opposing lineman. Muscle shoved against muscle. Seconds later the tempter picked himself off the grass. After the game he sought Bill out. "Lemme shake your hand, 'Crusher.' Your religion is as tough as your body block."

The big professional tackle is only one of many athletes who have come to respect Bill Krisher's muscles — both spiritual and physical. Only last year the "Crusher" stepped out of professional football to take the post of Associate Director of the Fellowship of Christian Athletes. A look at his record shows that Bill Krisher is well qualified to sign up sports champions for the greatest team of all coached by the Master Coach.

Seated at a desk in his Kansas City office Bill looks the part of a typical junior executive. But when he rises to meet you, the rippling muscles under his shirt betray his nickname — "Crusher." You realize that you are about to shake hands with a champion.

Bill's name has been familiar to pigskin fans since he burst on to sports pages as a sophomore guard for Oklahoma's 1955 National Champions. Coach Bud Wilkinson inserted Bill into the grid machine which was defeated only once during Bill's three seasons of varsity action. It was during his senior year that the "Crusher" blocked the extra point attempt by Colorado to help the Sooners hold on to their winning streak.

Bill was first nationally recognized in his junior year when *Sports Illustrated* chose him as a member of their All-American eleven. At the end of his senior year press organizations stood in line to hand him All-America honors. United Press, Associated Press, International News Service, *The Sporting News, Look* magazine, and NBC-TV all named him an All-American guard. After the season the "Crusher" played in the Orange Bowl, the Hula Bowl and the Senior Bowl — all in a month's time — and as one of the starters for the college all-stars against the National Football League champion Detroit Lions.

In professional football Bill has played in both the National Football League and the American Football League. He started with the Pittsburgh Steelers, then moved to the Dallas Texans. In 1960 he was a captain of the Texans, won All-Pro honors in the American Football League, and in 1961 played in the All-Star game of the AFL. Now as Associate Director of the Fellowship of Christian Athletes, Bill is in charge of personnel and athlete-led programs on college campuses.

"The FCA," Bill explains, "is a fellowship of Christian athletes, both active and retired, who believe that the Christian faith is practical, and that it really works in the stresses of life. We call it 'a program and movement to confront athletes — and through them the youth of the nation — with the challenge and adventure of the Christian life.'

"We are a non-profit organization governed by a board of directors of ministers and laymen formerly or presently active in athletics. Nationally famous coaches and professional athletes lead the inspirational and perspirational activities in our conferences — men like Paul Dietzel and Bob Petit.

"The FCA is evangelical in doctrine. In our conferences we challenge Christian athletes to go back home and become more active in their churches and to witness for Christ wherever they go."

As Bill Krisher leans over his desk, his piercing blue eyes reveal the purpose for which he and other Christian athletes are living. "An athlete understands the necessity of living under mastery and control," he continues. "He must control his body to be successful in the game. He must concentrate — control his mind — to excel. He cannot let his emotions rise up and take command in the midst of the stress that comes in serious competition. Likewise, in the more serious game of life, the Christian must find and experience the secret of control. This is only found when he commits himself — body, mind and spirit — to the Lordship of Christ."

Bill Krisher learned the secret of control when he was only ten. He accepted the Master Coach as his personal Savior during a revival conducted by Evangelist Hyman Appleman in the Exchange Avenue Baptist Church of Oklahoma City. Shortly afterward Bill's family moved to suburban Midwest City, Oklahoma, where they attended the First Baptist Church. Here Bill and his best friend, Don Nelson, quarterbacked the youth fellowship which met after Sunday evening services.

"Youth Fellowship and the church activities meant everything to me," Bill recalls fondly. "I experienced the joy of seeing young people come to Christ. I helped plan programs and devotions which turned out to be valuable preparation for my present work. I developed friendships with Christian youth which still endure today."

Today Bill talks with appreciation of the men who helped shape his life. First was his father, Irwin Krisher, a painter supervisor at Tinker Air Force Base. "Dad believed in taking me to Sunday school," Bill says. Then came his scoutmaster, A. V. Nelson, who took time to play with his scouts.

"Mr. Nelson was the father of my best friend," Bill says with a broad smile. "He was my ideal of what a Christian should be. I vividly remember an experience that happened when Don and I were in the eighth grade. We were rabbit hunting. I stopped to unload my gun and accidentally shot Don in the back. I was scared that Don might die when they took him to the hospital. But he recovered and through it all his dad understood that it was an accident. He held no hard feelings. He taught me the meaning of Christian love.

"My high school coach, Jake Spann, was tough, but good for me and the other boys. He challenged us to put out 100%

on the field. He enforced team discipline. We didn't dare be caught out after 10 P.M. He laid the law down about smoking and drinking. He encouraged us to ride a bike or walk to school — something a high school boy needs to do if he wants to develop into a first-class contender. Coach Spann was a man's man, but he was also our friend and counselor. He talked to us about dating and how we should respect girls' bodies. He led us to the state championship playoff in football, but more important, he made men out of us."

At the University of Oklahoma, Bill played on a champion team built by a champion coach, Bud Wilkinson. "Those days," Bill remembers, "everybody was talking about the unbeatable Oklahoma football team. The team went 47 games without a defeat. There were some great athletes at O.U. during those years. They were great because they were Christians. Almost every man on the team was a dedicated Christian. Just goes to show that Christian players can help a team win."

The big turning point in Bill's life came during his freshman year at the University of Oklahoma. During practice he fell, twisting his knee underneath his body. The team physician, Dr. O'Donohoe, took a cartilage out and then told Bill, "Four ligaments are torn loose from the bone. Looks like your football days are over."

After the doctor left, Bill stared up at the ceiling, contemplating his future. "I wondered what my life would be like without football," he now recalls. "I'd played since eighth grade. Could I sit on the sidelines while the other guys blocked, tackled and ran for touchdowns? I was a Christian then, but I asked myself, 'Am I living just to play football?' I decided that the only worthwhile purpose in life was to live for Christ. Right there, I promised to serve him with a smashed knee or with no knee at all. He had died for me. He had given me salvation, fellowship with Himself and assurance of eternal life. Why shouldn't I give all my life to Him?"

After the operation, Bill hobbled on crutches for eight weeks. During summer vacation he worked at a construction job, pouring heavy bags of cement even though his knee would only bend 30 degrees. He built up strength by riding a bike, lifting weights and working out every evening. "I wasn't sure I would ever play again," Bill says, "but I was going to try."

During Bill's sophomore year, Coach Wilkinson put him back into practice. The first week he broke a bone in his left hand. But Wilkinson did not lose confidence in him. He sent Bill in to play against North Carolina. Bill fell flat on his face as he ran out of the huddle. His team lined up without him. The opposing team laughed. But Bill got up, choked back the embarrassment and helped his team win a 7 to 6 decision. From this time on, Bill Krisher proved to be an All-American both in football and in the Christian life.

During his sophomore year Bill became active in the Fellowship of Christian Athletes movement. The FCA had been founded the year before by Don McClanen, a young basketball coach at Eastern Oklahoma A & M. Bill gave his testimony before college groups and in youth revivals. At the First Baptist Church of Norman, Oklahoma — home of OU — he served as associate superintendent of an Intermediate Sunday school department.

In January, 1961, Bill traveled to Guatamala with a group of Christian professional and businessmen under the auspices of *World Vision.* The men paid their own expenses. One day at a hotel Bill noticed a group of Portuguese athletes eating. "I could tell they were athletes," he says. "They were shoveling in the food with both hands."

Bill walked over to them and through an interpreter introduced himself. He learned they were the world soccer champion team from Brazil. Through the interpreter Bill and the Brazilians compared soccer to American football. "What are you doing here?" they asked Bill. This was his cue to give his Christian testimony. Afterward, one of the Brazilian athletes handed Bill a slip of paper on which he had written, "I like you."

Back in the states, Bill received several attractive offers to go into business. Several Christian organizations extended feelers. Bill finally chose to join the staff of the Fellowship of Christian Athletes. "I felt I could have more influence for Christ with the FCA through witnessing to athletes who knew me and in giving others an opportunity to witness through FCA," Bill says.

Today Bill is deeply concerned about reaching not only college and professional athletes, but also sports-minded, hero-worshiping youth. At 28, the handsome crew-cut ex-star fills his week-ends with speaking engagements in churches and in FCA conferences. The "Crusher" tells what Christ means to him and gives practical suggestions on how to live the life that wins. Naturally he uses illustrations from athletics.

"To succeed, a Christian must be a team man," Bill says. "Both in football and in the Christian life you must listen to other members of your team. For example, the guy next to me may say, 'Bill, move back a little — you're not lined up evenly.' I take his advice, otherwise I'm liable to be called offsides and cause my team to get a 5-yard penalty. We Christians must work together. We need each other. No one can run with the ball without the team backing him up.

"In football," Bill continues, "it's essential that a player know the mind of his coach and the players on the team. The practice field is important. A guy plays no better than he practices. In pro-football a player must learn over 400 plays to use against five or six defenses. He can't even average one mistake out of five and stay in pro-ball. We must get to know our Coach in the Christian life. We must learn the 'plays' He wants us to run. We do this through Bible study, prayer and fellowship with other Christians."

There's no doubt that Bill Krisher loves athletics — especially football. But for this muscle-man, living for Christ is a greater challenge. "You can be named an All-American football player and people will forget you two years later," Bill says. "But the life in Christ lasts forever and gives eternal joy. My goal in life is to be a witness for Him."

# 16

## BILL
## McCOLL, M.D.

The All-American Who Found
a Purpose in Living

**Medical Missionary: Taegu, Korea**
*All-American Stanford University,
1950-51; Star for Chicago Bears,
1952-59.*
*Home: San Jose, California*

DR. BILL McCOLL, the great Stanford end, is on his way to obscurity, for two years. He'll catch no passes in Korea." So said the *San Francisco Chronicle* when the twice All-American football player announced in the fall of 1962 that his lifetime Coach had led him to offer two years of his life for medical missions. Going with him will be his wife and six children.

The soft-spoken six-foot-four giant of 240 pounds was not even mildly aroused at the publicity given him by Chicago and San Francisco sports writers. Interviewed while packing, he explained simply: "Barbara and I are going to Korea for two years — and maybe a lifetime, because we have a desire to serve."

Bill McColl is one of the most storied athletes in Pacific Coast history. He has been known to throw 70-yard touchdown passes. By merely bumping into McColl, a San Jose player was knocked cold. And after a game in which Bill McColl caught seven passes for 108 yards and a game-winning touchdown, the Stanford coach, Marchie Schwartz, said longingly: "If a coach had 11 McColls all he'd need to do was

119

blow up the football." Coach Schwartz was thinking of Bill's little brother Johnny, also an All-American football player.

The McColls, who hail from Scotland, and more recently from California, have long been known as fighters. They trace their family lineage to the legendary Angus McColl, leader of a Highland Scottish clan. Sir Walter Scott lyrically related how big Angus McColl overcame a dozen MacPherson clansmen with his singing broadsword.

And in San Diego each year, the McColls get together for a reunion feast. Bill says, "By the time they all get there, there're more McColls in San Diego than sailors."

Like their clan, Bill McColl's family likes to do things together. Bill's father, whom he calls "Daddy" is a beloved community doctor who gave up sports to study medicine. As Bill and Johnny grew up — only two years apart — Dr. McColl made a small sports stadium out of their backyard. There was room and equipment for broad-jumping, pole-vaulting, high-jumping and even a basketball court and a crossbar for kicking football field goals. The enterprising doctor melted lead to mold 12-pound shots for the boys. And as the boys built up stamina and muscles, "Daddy" McColl hovered over them with pencil and notebook to record their performances.

One interesting note was made when Bill was only a toddler: "Bill ate a snail in the backyard today. Must check his digestion."

Today, Bill speaks endearingly of his father. "Daddy was a good doctor, but he never let medicine ruin his family. We laughed and played together and then on Sundays we went to Sunday school and church together at East San Diego Presbyterian Church."

As the boys grew up, "Daddy" McColl encouraged them to do their best in everything they tackled. Bill must have followed his advice. At 11, he won the San Diego Soapbox Derby title and the city-county kite-flying contest. He joined the Boy Scouts and in 15 months was ranked an Eagle Scout.

At Hoover High School in San Diego, Bill made the varsity football squad as a sophomore. But in the first game he broke his finger. "Daddy" McColl just happened to be team physician. He devised a special splint that held the finger rigid, then sent Bill back into the game.

Bill McColl became a school legend at Hoover High, eclipsing a former student, baseball star Ted Williams. He starred in football. In basketball he scored 398 points in his senior year. In baseball he hit .425 and struck out only three times in two years. He made the track team, although the school had trouble finding spiked shoes to fit Bill's size 14D feet.

Scholastically, he got almost an "A" average. He was elected President of the Boys Federation and Commissioner-General of the school, and was appointed student state police chief of California.

While Bill was looking for a university with a good medical school, the talent scouts were competing fiercely for his signature. Eighteen-year-old Bill was offered scholarships, grand campus tours, convertibles with gas for four years and one alumni group even offered to place on deposit a five-figure sum in any bank the McColls named. But Bill was not interested in their offers. One scout from a big name university admitted, "With Bill McColl, we were lucky not to get our noses jammed in the door."

Bill plainly told the subsidy hounds, "We McColls are not interested in getting something for nothing." Then he enrolled at Stanford after receiving a competitive scholastic scholarship.

At Stanford, Bill racked up "A's" in the classroom and touchdowns on the football field. In 1951 Bill McColl led the Stanford Redskins to nine straight victories and a bid to the Rose Bowl. He was named All-American during both his junior and senior years (1950-51). His picture appeared on the covers of three national U. S. magazines. The Helms Athletic Foundation of Los Angeles selected him as the college football player of the year. United Press elected him "lineman of the year."

As in high school, long before Bill got his college diploma, the scouts were buzzing about him like flies on honey. The manager of the Chicago Bears told his scout: "Do anything, make any deal you need to make — but get the draft rights to McColl."

Bill frankly told the scouts that "My medical career comes first. But," he added, "I might play pro-football if I could also go to medical school."

The Chicago Bears agreed to make this unusual concession. In 1952 Bill signed their team roster and enrolled at the University of Chicago medical school. He played professional football from 1952-59 and gave his usual star performance. During this time he also acquired his medical degree and wife Barbara, his Stanford sweetheart.

In 1958 he was admitted as a resident in orthopedic surgery at the University of Illinois Research and Educational Hospital. In 1962 he was certified as an orthopedic surgeon. This same year he departed for Korea to serve a two-year stint in medical missions.

When asked why he is delaying his career as a surgeon to serve in a mission hospital, Dr. Bill reverently referred to the "biggest commitment I ever made."

Four years ago Bill took his family to a church family camp in Saugatuck, Michigan. "There," he says, "I realized I had been living on secondhand Christianity. I had been taught the Christian faith from childhood, but had never committed my life to Christ. I heard a speaker say, 'It doesn't take much of a man to become a Christian, but it takes all of him.'

"I began re-evaluating my purpose in life. I thought of my responsibilities as a father to my children. I felt that the most important thing I could give them was the example of a Christian father who would instill Christian principles into their lives. My commitment was not especially dramatic, but it was real."

After returning from the camp, Bill became active in the First Presbyterian Church of Oak Park, Illinois. He began teaching his children the "principles of the Christian faith." "Then," he said, "after I saw the rewards of teaching my children, I offered to teach a Sunday school class of young boys."

As Dr. Bill continued his surgical training he began to

think more about his future as a doctor. "I had originally planned to return to California," he said, "but now I began asking myself if this was what God wanted me to do."

Dr. Bill and Barbara talked about their future in family council. They prayed. Then came the idea. Why not offer themselves to a mission board for two years' service in a mission field? While serving the needy, in a Christian mission community, they could plan their future.

They established a basic criteria for the selection of a mission hospital: Bill must be able to utilize his specialized orthopedic training; education facilities must be available for the children; we will commit ourselves for only two years, with the possibility of an extension.

Setting forth these criteria, Dr. Bill began corresponding with mission boards. Almost every answer was the same: "The expense would be too great. Your wife would have difficulty adjusting with six small children. We cannot accept you on a temporary basis."

Dr. Bill explained that he was not sure of a "call" to lifetime medical missions. But he would give two years of his life and during that time he would seek God's leadership while serving. Still, repeated correspondence brought more negative replies.

They gave up the idea and began making definite plans to set up practice in California. But a Presbyterian minister friend, the Rev. John Burton, felt something still could be done. He contacted Dr. Howard Moffett, a medical missionary on furlough from the Presbyterian Hospital in Taegu, Korea. Dr. Moffett spelled out the hospital's need for an orthopedic surgeon to replace the regular orthopedist who had gone to India for special study.

Mr. Burton brought Dr. McColl and Dr. Moffett together. Then he asked: "If we raise your support locally, will you still go?" Dr. Bill talked with Barbara. "Yes," they replied enthusiastically.

Mr. Burton led in organizing a committee to raise pledges for the McColl Korea Fund. Then he wrote his denominational mission board (United Presbyterian) in behalf of the

McColls. "We will raise the money locally for their support, if the board will endorse their service," he proposed.

The board accepted. The necessary funds were raised. In June 1962 Dr. Bill McColl finished his residency in orthopedic surgery. The following month the McColls with their six children — Duncan 6, twins Carrie and Bonnie 5½, John 4½, Milton 2½ and Jennifer 1 — packed for Korea.

Before leaving, Dr. Bill was asked if he thought work would be more exciting for him than playing football. "This will be different," he said. "I enjoyed playing football and I expect to enjoy missionary medicine. This will be more of a challenge and I expect each day to be more exciting than the day before.

"We'll live in a missionary compound with 18 doctors. I'll be one of just two or three American doctors in the group. There is a tremendous need for an orthopedic surgeon in Korea. There is osteomylitis, which is the bone disease suffered by Mickey Mantle; there are many injuries from children stepping on land mines and grenades remaining from the Korean War. Many Korean children have frozen and frostbitten feet. We will have many amputations. We will also do reconstructive work among lepers and try to repair what this disease has ravaged."

A recent report from Korea shows that Dr. Bill is busy in the challenging work of medical missions. In a typical week he performs six to ten major operations besides teaching Korean doctors and nurses. He has paid from his own missionary salary the medical expenses of some patients who otherwise could not have afforded an operation.

He manages to find time to hold sick call in the poorer sections of Taegu. Once a week he calls at Sungbo-won orphanage, where he ministers to crippled children.

Even in Korea he hasn't given up football. He is now organizing a Korean football league which looks very promising.

Busy in his chosen work, Dr. Bill has little time to philosophize. But perhaps he best summed up his reason for going before he left Chicago when he said, "We have a desire to serve."

# CONCLUSION

## HOW TO WIN THE GAME OF LIFE

Now THAT YOU have read these inspiring stories you may be asking, "How can I win the game of life?" After all, this is one game we're all in, and in this game the rewards to the winners and the penalties to the losers are of everlasting significance.

Here are a few suggestions . . . .

FIRST: *Join the winning team coached by the Master Coach, Jesus Christ.*

How do you get a uniform? Not the way baseball and football players do. They qualify because of their record, ability and skill. But when it comes to joining the Christian team, your record or ability does not count. The Master Coach wants to take you as you are and start from the ground up and build you into a champion. No amount of bragging about your good life will impress Him. He will give you a "uniform of righteousness" only when you admit your unrighteousness and put your faith in Him.

SECOND: *Make a commitment to win.*

Paul Dietzel, Bill Wade, Bobby Richardson and other great Christian athletes are playing to win. There is no half-heartedness about these fellows. They are winning athletic contests and the game of life because they are playing with the purpose of winning.

THIRD: *Follow the Rule Book.*

One man offsides can penalize a football team. Failure to touch a base can cost a baseball team a run and perhaps a game. By skirting the rules you can penalize the whole Christian team, especially the local fellowship of Christians to which you belong.

The Bible is the Rule Book for the Christian Team. You will find here directions for running the "plays" of life. Here you will be warned about the tricks of the opposition and given instructions on how to avoid his "fakes." Here, also, you will find instructions for training — how to pray, witness and play victoriously on the field of life.

FOURTH: *Follow the Coach's directions.*

How will Christ, your Coach, direct you? Through the Bible, our Rule Book; through the Holy Spirit, the inward Voice living within every Christian; through assistant coaches, such as pastors, Sunday school teachers, and other Christian leaders.

FIFTH: *Keep in training.*

Football pass receivers squeeze putty to keep their hands strong. Baseball pitchers work out before every game they pitch. Exercises and a proper diet are the order of every athlete's day, along with game films which show up weak points in last week's game.

Athletes also scan game films showing their opponents in action. What kind of a ball does a certain pitcher throw? What fakes does a pass receiver use when running a pass pattern? To win, a team must know the strategy of their opponents.

It is so in the Christian game of life. There are no substitutes for the spiritual disciplines of Bible study, prayer, witnessing, self-sacrifice and fellowship with other Christians. We must know the strategy of the great "deceiver" or else he may throw us for a loss. We must know and take steps to correct weak points, such as anger, covetousness, discouragement, impatience, etc.

SIXTH: *Learn to take setbacks.*

The best football quarterback is sometimes thrown for a loss. Even the great Babe Ruth struck out more than once. A champion contender expects to suffer humiliation and loss of face. But after each setback, he gets up and gets back in the game.

As a member of the Christian team, you can expect to be tackled by the evil team and sometimes thrown for a loss. But you can get up and get back into the game of life, remembering the promise, "There hath no temptation (trial) taken you but such as is common to man: but God is faithful, who will not suffer (permit) you to be tempted above that ye are able: but will with the temptation (trial) also make a way of escape that ye may be able to bear it" (I Corinthians 10:13).

SEVENTH: *Be a team man.*

When the quarterback fades back to pass he depends upon his linemen to form a protective pocket around him and keep "red dogging" tacklers away. In all team sports, teamwork is essential. No player can win a game by himself.

In the game of life we must pull together under the direction of Christ. Only a few can be quarterbacks or ends who run with the ball. Most of us must hold the line and back up the ball carriers. The success of our team depends upon each member doing his part. We must pull together or the opponent will pull us apart.

EIGHTH: *Keep your eyes on the goal.*

A champion team plays to score, for only by scoring can a team win a pennant or a world's championship.

On the Christian team we run to secure the commendation of God. We strive to hear Him say, "Well done, thou good and faithful servant." This will be reward enough for us when the game of life is over.

The Apostle Paul was a star performer on the Christian team. He used the language of the sports arena in declaring his goal in life: "I press toward the mark for the prize of the high calling of God" (Philippians 3:14).

He fully expected to reach his goal for he said just before his death, "I have fought a good fight, I have finished my course, I have kept the faith: Henceforth there is laid up for me a crown of righteousness" (II Timothy 4:7, 8).